MESS...
the promi...
journal
STACEY MARTIN

See back inside page for convenient reading checklist that may be copied.

Messiah Revealed: The Promise of The Ages Journal
© 2018 by Stacey Martin (print and photos)

All rights reserved. No part of this publication may be reproduced in any form without written permission from Book Villages, P.O. Box 64526, Colorado Springs, CO 80962. www.bookvillages.com

ISBN: 978-1-94429-844-9

Cover Design, Interior Design and Layout by Dennis Humphrey and Bethany Zalman

Scripture quotations marked (AMP) are taken from the AMPLIFIED Bible, Copyright © 1954, 1958, 1962, 1964, 1964, 1987 by The Lockman Foundation. All rights reserved. Used by permission. www.Lockman.org

Scripture quotations marked (NASB) are taken from the NEW AMERICAN STANDARD BIBLE®, Copyright © 1960, 1962, 1963, 1968, 1972, 1973, 1975, 1977, 1995 The Lockman Foundation. Used by permission.

Scripture quotations marked (NIV) are taken from the HOLY BIBLE, NEW INTERNATIONAL VERSION®. Copyright © 1973, 1978, 1984 by International Bible Society. Used by permission of Zondervan Publishing House. All rights reserved.
The "NIV" and "New International Version" trademarks are registered in the United States Patent and Trademark Office by International Bible Society. Use of either trademark requires the permission of International Bible Society.

Scripture quotations marked NLT are taken from the Holy Bible, New Living Translation, copyright © 1996, 2004, 2007, 2013 by Tyndale House Foundation. Used by permission of Tyndale House Publishers, Inc., Carol Stream, Illinois 60188. All rights reserved.

Printed in the United States of America
1 2 3 4 5 6 7 8 printing/year 22 21 20 19 18

How To Use this Bible Reading Guide:

Read through the Bible in segments of chapters (363 reading segments) at a personal pace.
Each text box has:
• the **Reading Segment Title**
• a **Passage** of that reading segment
• and a **Connection** reference

• **Reading Segment Titles:** Reading segment titles are in **Large Bold Type** (whether Old or New Testament) and are located at the top of each text box.

• **Passages:** Passages are in **(parentheses)**. Old Testament passages within Old Testament reading segments refer to related New Testament connections. Likewise, New Testament passages within the New Testament reading segments refer to Old Testament connections.

• **Connections:** Connections are in "quotes." Old Testament and New Testament connections are in quotes under the passages.
For example, Reading Segment 147:
• the **Reading Segment Title** of 147 is:
1 Chronicles 1-3

• the **Passage** of reading segment 147 is:
(1 Ch 2:9-15)

• the **Connection** reference of 147 is:
Mt 1:1; a New Testament connection with the Old Testament passage of (1 Ch 2:9-15)

Photos:
Each Photo was taken on location in the Holyland and represents a reference found within its reading segment.

Journal Space:
The background for the journal space is a photo of the southern wall of Jerusalem's Temple Mount.

Genesis 1-3
(Ge 1:3)

"For God who said, let light shine out of darkness, has shone in our hearts..."
2 Co 4:6 (AMP)

Ge 1:5 Evening fishing at the Sea of Galilee

Genesis 4-6
(Ge 4:14, 15)

"There will no longer be any curse...they will see His face..." Rv 22:3, 4
"...the glory of God in the face of Christ." 2Co 4:6 (NASB)

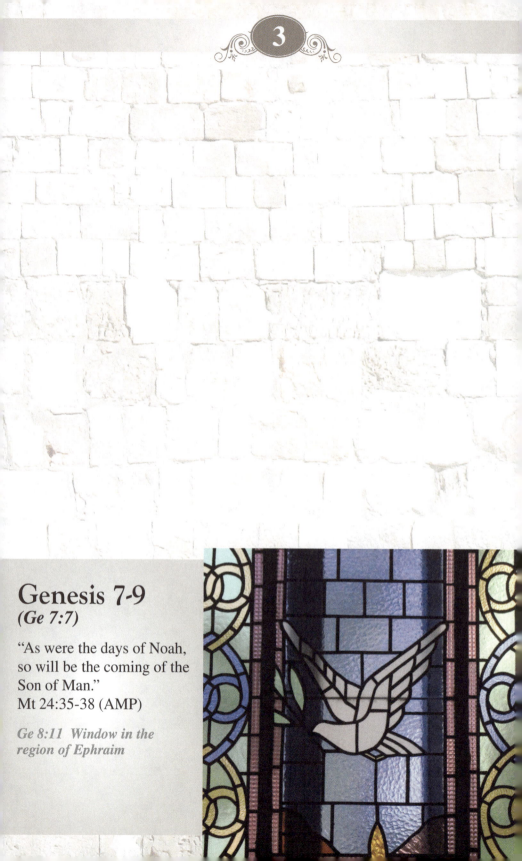

Genesis 7-9
(Ge 7:7)

"As were the days of Noah, so will be the coming of the Son of Man."
Mt 24:35-38 (AMP)

Ge 8:11 Window in the region of Ephraim

Genesis 10-11
(Ge 10:32)

" '...You...purchased for God with Your blood... every tribe and tongue and people and nation.' "
Rev 5:6-9 (NASB)

Ac 17:26, 27
Ethiopian in Jerusalem

5

Genesis 12-16
(Ge 12:3)

"...God proclaimed this good news to Abraham long ago..." Gal 3:8 [Eph 3:4-9] (NLT)

Bedouin tent-dweller

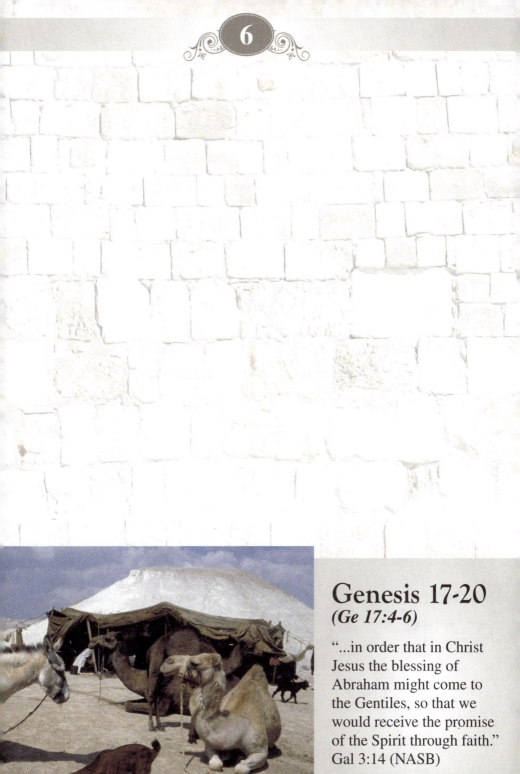

Genesis 17-20
(Ge 17:4-6)

"...in order that in Christ Jesus the blessing of Abraham might come to the Gentiles, so that we would receive the promise of the Spirit through faith."
Gal 3:14 (NASB)

*Ge 18:1
Sitting at the tent door*

7

Genesis 21-24:10
(Ge 22:18)

"...And to your Seed... referring to one individual..."
Gal 3:16-18 (AMP)

Ge 21:30
Lambs in Nazareth

8

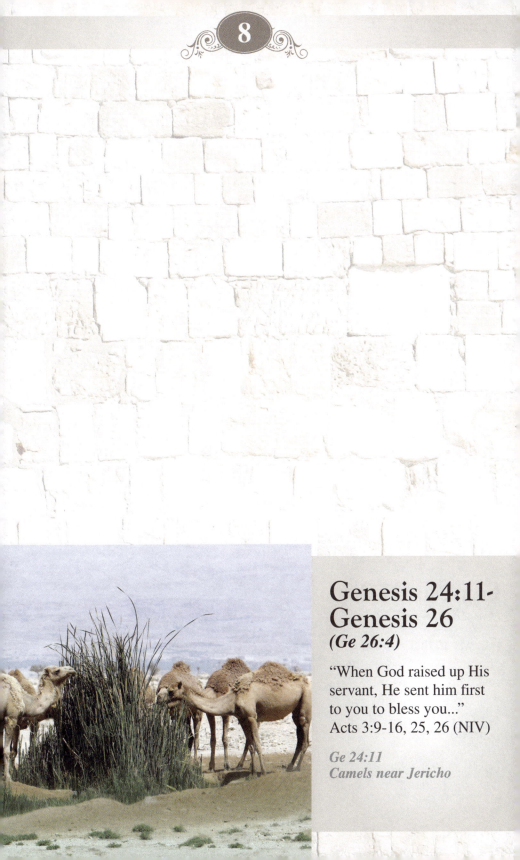

Genesis 24:11- Genesis 26
(Ge 26:4)

"When God raised up His servant, He sent him first to you to bless you..."
Acts 3:9-16, 25, 26 (NIV)

Ge 24:11
Camels near Jericho

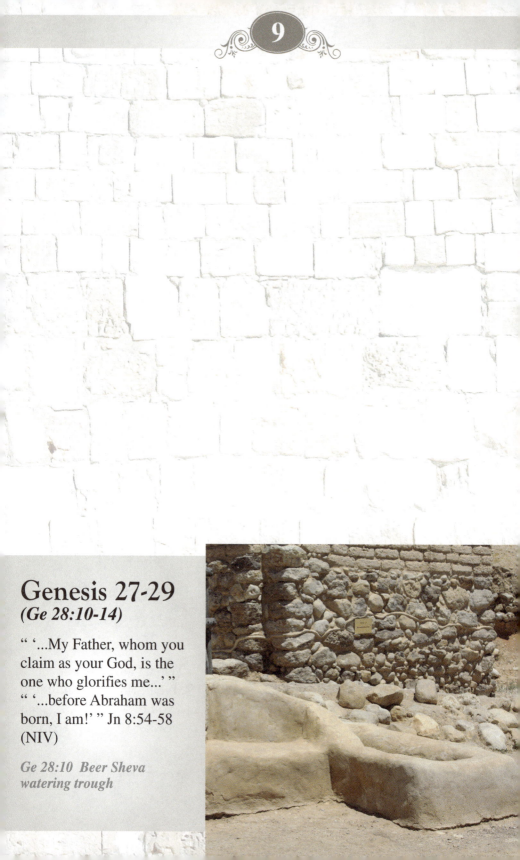

Genesis 27-29
(Ge 28:10-14)

" '...My Father, whom you claim as your God, is the one who glorifies me...' "
" '...before Abraham was born, I am!' " Jn 8:54-58 (NIV)

Ge 28:10 Beer Sheva watering trough

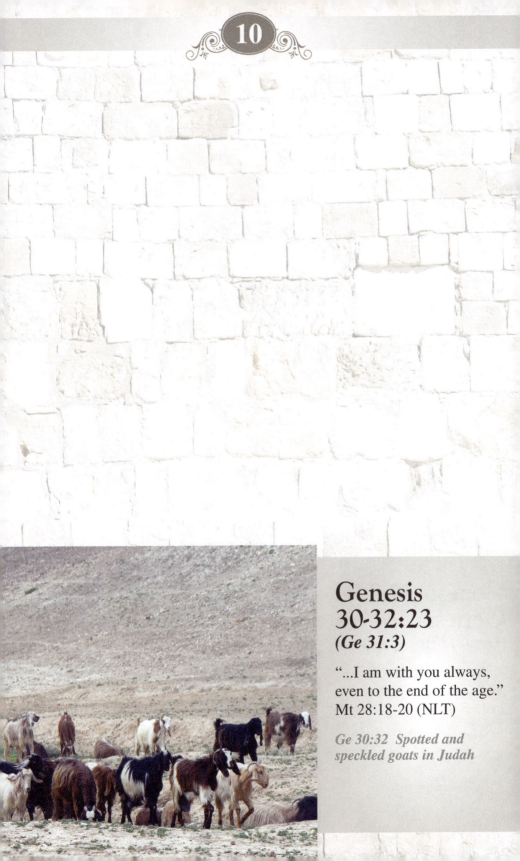

Genesis 30-32:23
(Ge 31:3)

"...I am with you always, even to the end of the age."
Mt 28:18-20 (NLT)

Ge 30:32 Spotted and speckled goats in Judah

11

Genesis 32:24 - Genesis 35
(Ge 32:30)

"...Anyone who has seen Me has seen the Father..." Jn 14:8-11 (AMP)

Ge 33:13 Young sheep

12

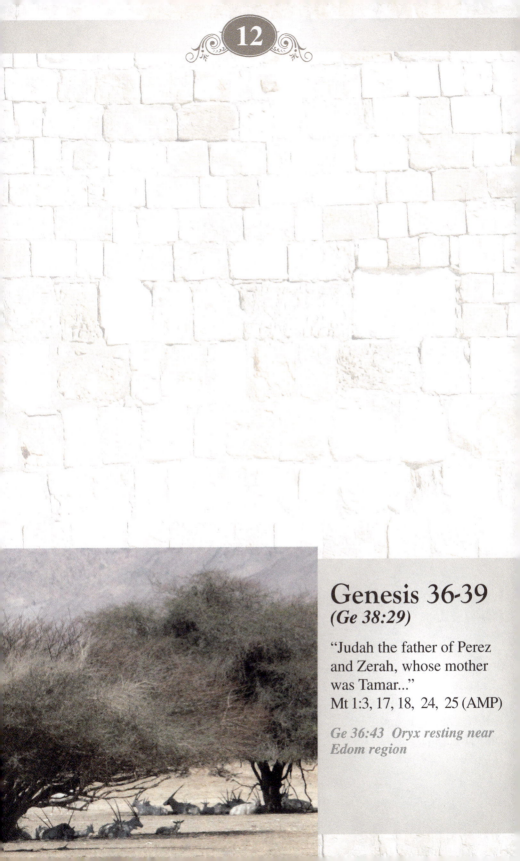

Genesis 36-39
(Ge 38:29)

"Judah the father of Perez and Zerah, whose mother was Tamar..."
Mt 1:3, 17, 18, 24, 25 (AMP)

Ge 36:43 Oryx resting near Edom region

13

Genesis 40-43
(Ge 41:25)

"...appeared to him in a dream, saying, 'Joseph, son of David...' " " '...she will bear a Son; and you shall call His name Jesus...' "
Mt 1:18-23 [Isa 7:14] (NASB)

Ge 42:26
Woman leading donkey

14

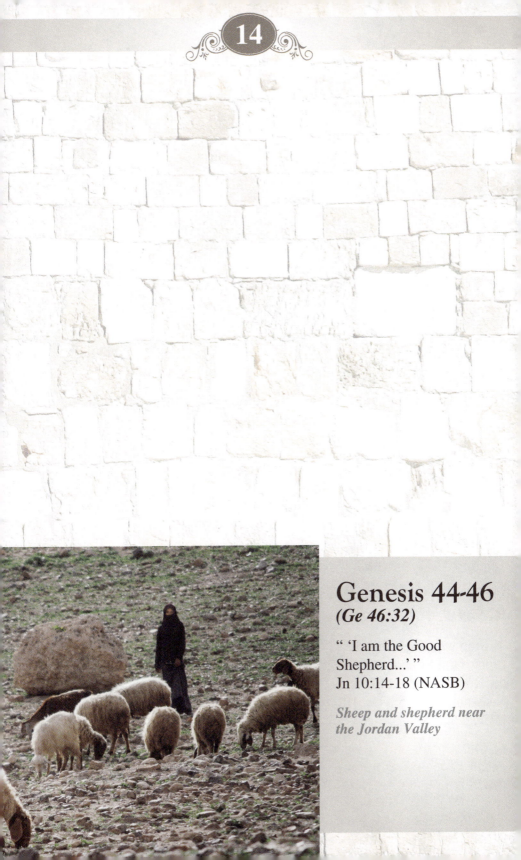

Genesis 44-46
(Ge 46:32)

" 'I am the Good Shepherd...' "
Jn 10:14-18 (NASB)

Sheep and shepherd near the Jordan Valley

Genesis 47-50
(Ge 49:9, 10)

"...Stop weeping! See, the Lion of the tribe of Judah, the Root (Source) of David, has won...!" Rv 5:5 (AMP) [Micah 5:2; Mt 2:4-6]

Ge 47:13
Yellow Chamomile growing in parched ground near the Dead Sea, responding to early rains

Job 1-4
(Jb 4:17)

"...Then God made you alive with Christ, for he forgave all our sins. He canceled the record of the charges against us..." Col 2:9-14 (NLT)

Jb 1:3
Female donkey near Jericho

Job 5-7
(Jb 5:13)

"...they were amazed with bewildered wonder, and said, Where did this Man get this wisdom...?"
Mt 13:53, 54 (AMP)

Jb 5:10
Rain on Bethpage

Job 8-10
(Jb 9:15)

"And His mercy (His compassion and kindness toward the miserable and afflicted) is on those who fear Him..."
Lk 1:46-50 (AMP)

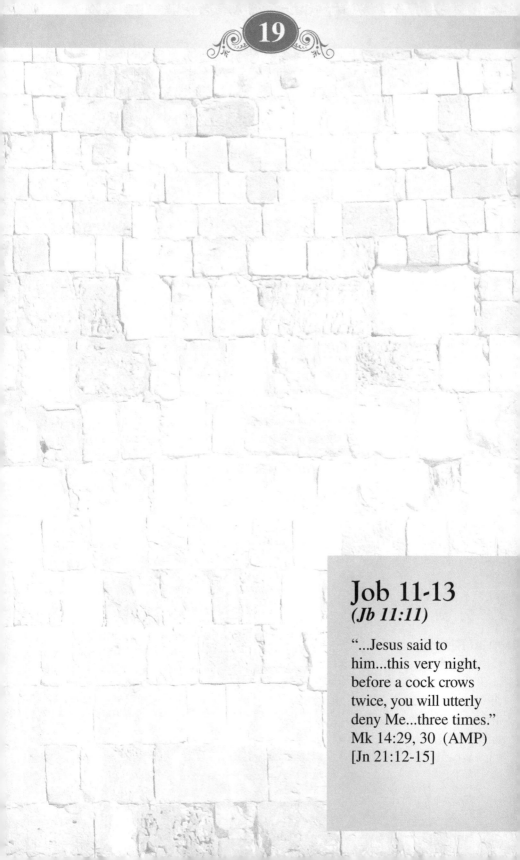

Job 11-13
(Jb 11:11)

"...Jesus said to him...this very night, before a cock crows twice, you will utterly deny Me...three times." Mk 14:29, 30 (AMP) [Jn 21:12-15]

Job 14-17
(Jb 16:2)

"...so also our comfort is abundant through Christ." 2Co 1:3-5 (NASB)

Jb 14:7 Eastern Strawberry Tree shoot, Jerusalem

21

Job 18-20
(Jb 19:25)

"...being justified as a gift by His grace through the redemption which is in Christ Jesus..." Ro 3:24 (NASB) [Jn 1:29]

Job 21-24
(Jb 23:5)

Jesus speaks: " '...Let me teach you, because I am gentle and humble at heart, and you will find rest for your souls.' " Mt 11:28-30 (NLT)

Mt 11:29 "gentle and humble" Young Bedouin with baby donkey

Job 25-28
(Jb 26:12)

" '...Who is this man?' they asked each other. 'Even the wind and waves obey him!' "
Mk 4:35-41 (NLT)

Mk 4:41 Sea of Galilee

24

Job 29 -31
(Jb 30:27)

"Do not let your hearts be troubled (distressed, agitated). You...rely on God...rely also on Me." Jn 14:1 (AMP)

Jb 29:23 Spring, Jerusalem hillside

25

Job 32-34
(Jb 32:8)

"...understanding... that they may know the mystery of God, namely, Christ, in whom are hidden all treasures of wisdom and knowledge."
Col 2:2, 3 (NIV)
[Lk 2:46-49; 1Jn 5:20]

26

Job 35-38
(Jb 36:22)

"...Jesus said...But you are not to be called rabbi (teacher), for you have one Teacher..."
Mt 23:1, 8 (AMP)

Jb 38:27 "...to cause the tender grass to spring forth..."

Job 39-42
(Jb 42:1, 2)

"...Lord...grant that Your bond-servants may speak... while You extend Your hand to heal, and signs and wonders take place through the name of Your holy servant, Jesus."
Ac 4:13, 23-31 (AMP)
[Ps 2:1, 2]

Jb 39:5, 6 Persian Wild Donkey north of Elat

Exodus 1-4
(Ex 3:10)

Stephen speaks: "This is that Moses who told the Israelites, 'God will send you a prophet like me from your own people.' " Ac 7:35, 37 [Jn 6:4-14] (NIV)

Ex 3:8 "...milk and honey..." Bee at Juda's Tree blossoms, Jerusalem

Exodus 5-8
(Ex 6:2, 5, 6)

"...you were...strangers to the covenants..."
"...But now in Christ Jesus you who formerly were far off have been brought near..." Eph 2:11-13
"...to Jesus, the mediator of a new covenant..." Heb 12:22-24 (NASB)

Ex 6:8 "...I will bring You..."
Northern Sea of Galilee

Exodus 9-11
(Ex 11:2)

"For you know that it was not with perishable things such as silver or gold that you were redeemed..."
1Pe 1:18-21 (NIV)

Ex 10:26 "Our livestock too must go with us..."
Flock between Jerusalem and Jericho

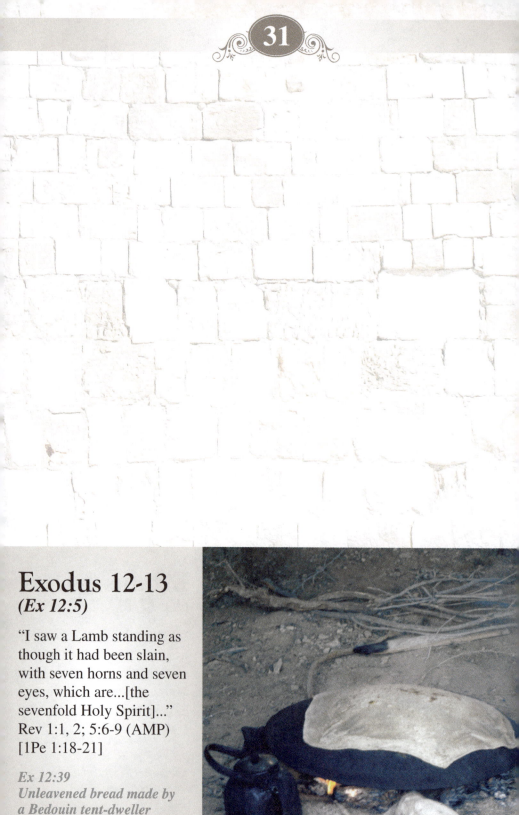

Exodus 12-13
(Ex 12:5)

"I saw a Lamb standing as though it had been slain, with seven horns and seven eyes, which are...[the sevenfold Holy Spirit]..." Rev 1:1, 2; 5:6-9 (AMP) [1Pe 1:18-21]

Ex 12:39
Unleavened bread made by a Bedouin tent-dweller

32

Exodus 14-15
(Ex 14:13)

Jesus speaking: "...He has anointed Me [the Anointed One, the Messiah] to preach the good news...to announce release to the captives..." Lk 4:17-21 (AMP)
[Is 61:1, 2; Ro 8:2, 15]

Ex 15:27 Palm trees

33

Exodus 16-18
(Ex 16:32)

"...I [Myself] am this Living Bread that came down from heaven." Jn 6:41-51 (AMP)

Tent-dwelling, Bedouin women making bread near the Dead Sea

34

Exodus 19-22
(Ex 19:9)

Jesus answers: "But blessed...are your...ears because they do hear...many prophets and righteous men ...yearned to see what you see...and hear what you hear..." Mt 13:16, 17 (AMP)

Ex 22:9
Donkey with flock

35

Exodus 23-27
(Ex 25:8, 9, 40)

"...He entered the holy place once for all, having obtained eternal redemption."
Heb 3:1-6; 9:10-12 (NASB)

Ex 23:12
" '...on the seventh day you shall cease from labor...' "
A new day starting

Exodus 28-29
(Ex 28:36-38)

"For we do not have a high priest who cannot sympathize with our weaknesses..." "Therefore let us draw near with confidence to the throne of grace..."
Heb 4:12-16 (NASB)

Ex 28:33 Pomegranates growing in Jerusalem

Exodus 30-33
(Ex 32:16; Jer 31:33)

"...you are a letter from Christ...not written with ink but with [the] Spirit of [the] living God, not on tablets of stone but on tablets of human hearts."
2Co 3:3 [Heb 8:10] (AMP)

Ex 30:1 Nubian Ibex walking on Acacia tree at Ein Gedi

38

Exodus 34-36
(Ex 36:35; Ex 26:33)

"Then Jesus...released his spirit. At that moment the curtain in the sanctuary of the Temple was torn in two, from top to bottom..." Mt 27:50, 51 (NLT)

Ex 34:18
"...month of Abib..."
(or Aviv) Spring on the Mount of Olives

Exodus 37-40
(Ex 39:32)

"For Christ did not enter into a holy place made with human hands, which was only a copy of the true one in heaven. He entered into heaven itself to appear now before God on our behalf."
Heb 9:24 (NLT)

Ex 37:1 Acacia tree, Ein Gedi

Leviticus 1-4
(Lv 4:3)

"He sacrificed for their sins once for all when He offered Himself."
Heb 7:23-27 (NIV)

Lv 2:1 Frankincense at Jerusalem market

Leviticus 5-7
(Lv 6:4, 5)

"...if I have cheated anyone ...I [now] restore four times..." "And Jesus said... Today is...salvation come...For the Son of Man came to seek and to save that which was lost."
Lk 19:1-10 (AMP)

Leviticus 8-9
(Lv 8:27, 28)

"...offerings you have not desired, but instead You have made ready a body for Me [to offer]..." "...we have been made holy...through the offering made once for all..." Heb 10:3-10 (AMP) [Ps 40:6-8]

Leviticus 10-13
(Lv 12:6-8)

"...according to the law of Moses...they brought Him up to Jerusalem..."
About Simeon: "...the Holy Spirit...revealed...he would not see death before he had seen the Lord's Christ."
Lk 2:21-32 (NASB)

Lv 11:4 Camels in palm grove

Leviticus 14-16:25
(Lv 14:1, 2)

Jesus said: " 'I am willing; be cleansed...' " " '...go, show yourself to the priest and present the offering that Moses commanded, as a testimony to them.' "
Mt 8:1-4 (NASB)

Lv 16:4 Linen turban of Samaritan priest

Leviticus 16:26-19:11
(Lv 16:27)

"...Jesus also suffered and died outside the [city's] gate in order that He might purify and consecrate the people..." Heb 13:11, 12 (AMP)

Lv 19:3 "...give due respect..." Bedouin mother and child

Leviticus 19:12-21:24
(Lv 19:18, 34)

"...love the Lord your God with all your heart... and love your neighbor as yourself." Lk 10:25-28
"...not that we loved God, but that He loved us and sent His Son to be the propitiation...for our sins." 1Jn 4:7-10 (AMP)

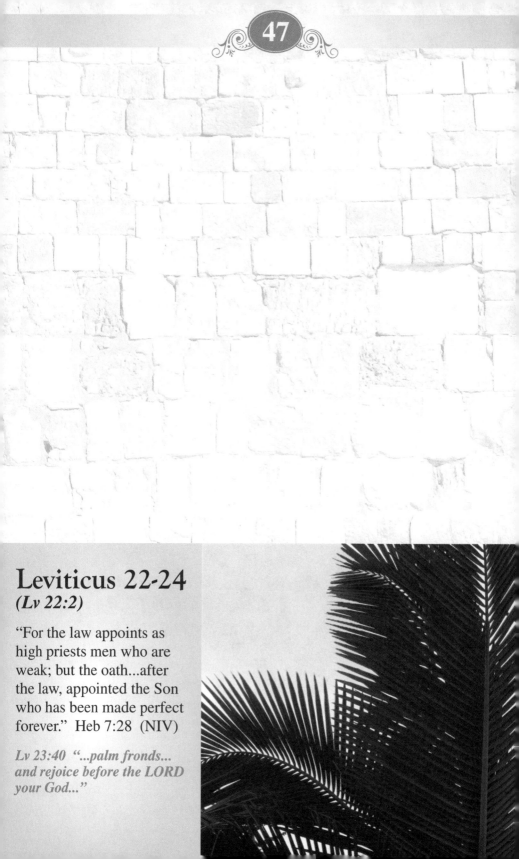

Leviticus 22-24
(Lv 22:2)

"For the law appoints as high priests men who are weak; but the oath...after the law, appointed the Son who has been made perfect forever." Heb 7:28 (NIV)

Lv 23:40 "...palm fronds... and rejoice before the LORD your God..."

Leviticus 25-27
(Lv 25:23)

"...you are...strangers and temporary residents with Me." Lv 25:23
"...I say [exactly] what My Father has taught Me. And He who sent Me is ever with Me..." Jn 8:19, 28, 29 (AMP)
[*Abraham:* Heb 11:9, 10, 13]

Lv 26:4 Bee at fig tree

Numbers 1-5
(Num 4:17-20)

"...as we have a great High Priest...Jesus the Son of God..." "Let us then...boldly draw near to the throne of grace..." Heb 4:14-16 (AMP) [Heb 6:19, 20; Mk 15:37, 38; Lk 23:44, 45]

Numbers 6-10
(Num 9:1, 2, 12)

"...I saw a Lamb standing, as though it had been slain, with seven horns and with seven eyes, which are the seven Spirits of God [the sevenfold Holy Spirit]..."
Rv 5:6-9 (AMP)
[Is 53:7; Jn 19:30, 33, 36]

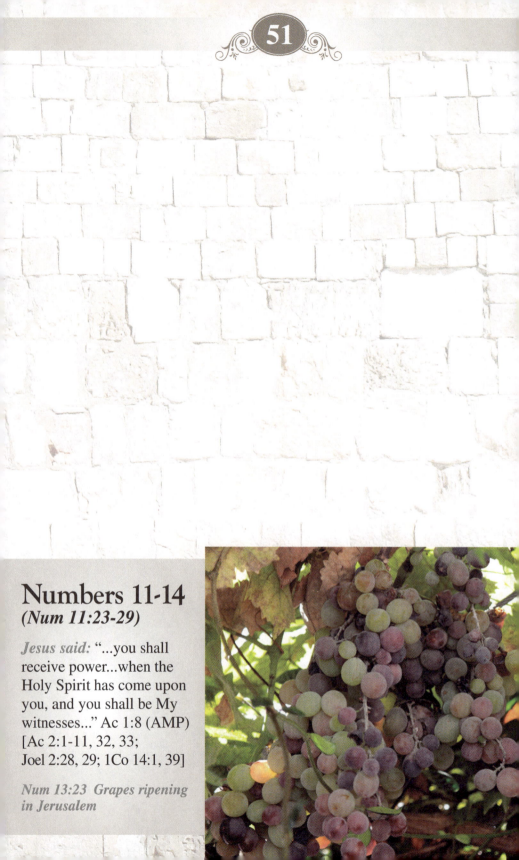

Numbers 11-14
(Num 11:23-29)

Jesus said: "...you shall receive power...when the Holy Spirit has come upon you, and you shall be My witnesses..." Ac 1:8 (AMP) [Ac 2:1-11, 32, 33; Joel 2:28, 29; 1Co 14:1, 39]

Num 13:23 Grapes ripening in Jerusalem

Numbers 15-17
(Num 15:26)

"...we through the Spirit, by faith, are waiting for the hope of righteousness. For in Christ Jesus neither cirumcision nor uncircumcision means anything, but faith working through love." Gal 5:5, 6 (NASB)

Num 17:8 Ripe almonds

Numbers 18-20
(Num 20:8)

"...tell the rock...to give forth its water..." Num 20:8
"...the Rock was Christ."
1Co 10:1-4 (AMP)
[Jn 7:2, 37, 38; 4:7-14]

*Num 20:1; 33:36
Kadesh, Ibex in the
Zin Wilderness*

54

Numbers 21-23
(Num 21:8)

" 'Just as Moses lifted up the snake in the desert, so the Son of Man must be lifted up.' "
" '...not...to condemn... but to save the world through him.' "
Jn 3:13-17 (NIV)

55

Numbers 24-27
(Num 24:1, 2, 12, 13, 17)

" '...We saw his star in the east and have come to worship him.' "
Mt 2:1, 2, 9-12 (NIV)

Numbers 28-30
(Num 28:9, 10)

" '...there is one here who is even greater than the Temple!...' "
" 'For the Son of Man is Lord even over the Sabbath!' "
Mt 12:5-8 (NLT)

Numbers 31-33
(Num 31:49)

"And this is the will of Him Who sent Me, that I should not lose any of all that He has given Me, but that I should give new life and raise [them all] up at the last day."
Jn 6:35-40 (AMP)

Bedouin boy with young lamb

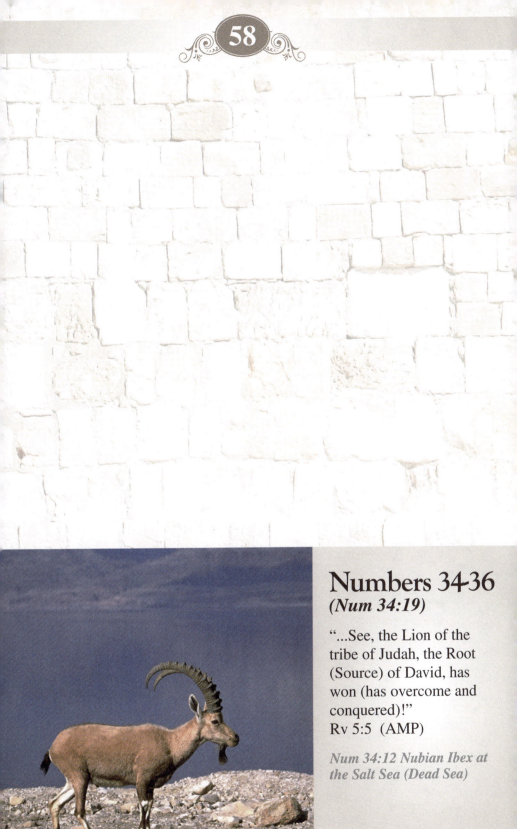

Numbers 34-36
(Num 34:19)

"...See, the Lion of the tribe of Judah, the Root (Source) of David, has won (has overcome and conquered)!"
Rv 5:5 (AMP)

Num 34:12 Nubian Ibex at the Salt Sea (Dead Sea)

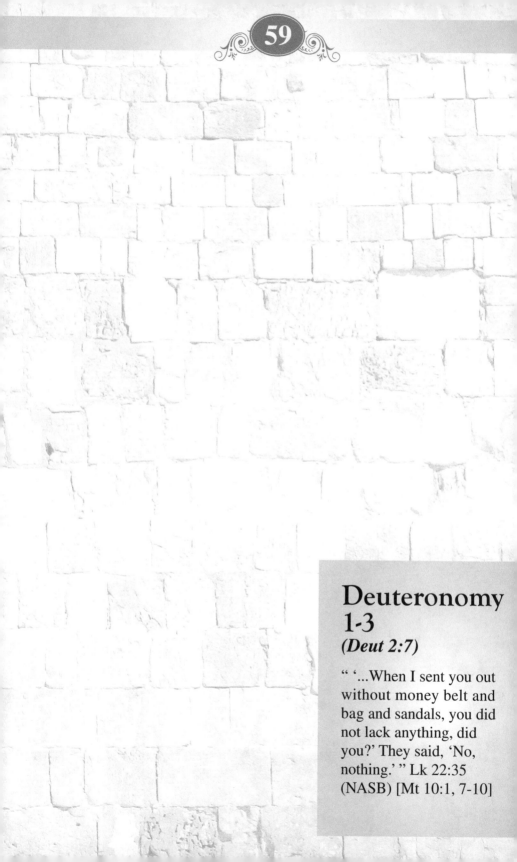

Deuteronomy 1-3
(Deut 2:7)

" '...When I sent you out without money belt and bag and sandals, you did not lack anything, did you?' They said, 'No, nothing.' " Lk 22:35 (NASB) [Mt 10:1, 7-10]

Deuteronomy 4-6
(Deut 6:4)

" 'I and the Father are one.' "
Jn 10:25-30 (NASB)

Deut 4:49 Gazelle in the "...Arabah..." or Aravah

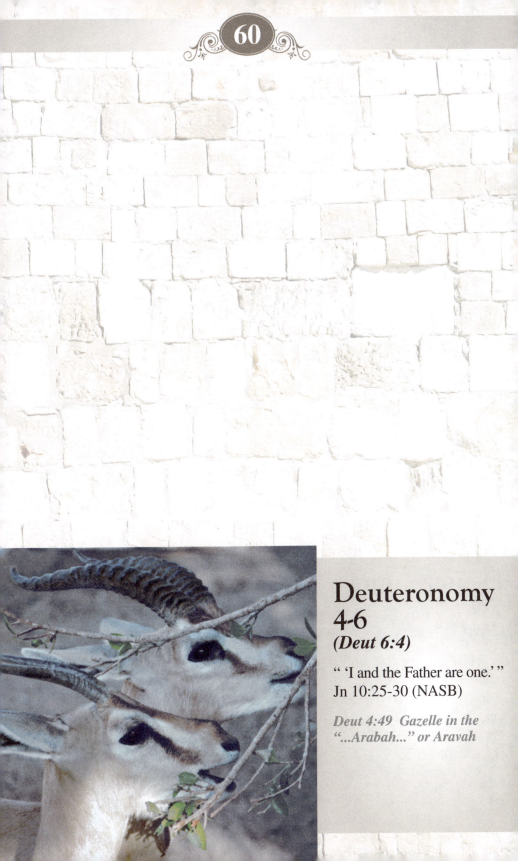

Deuteronomy 7-9
(Deut 7:8)

"...when the time had fully come, God sent his Son, born of a woman, born under law, to redeem those under law..." Gal 4:1-6 (NIV) [Lk 24:15, 21, 26, 27]

Deut 8:9 "*...you can dig copper out of the hills.*"

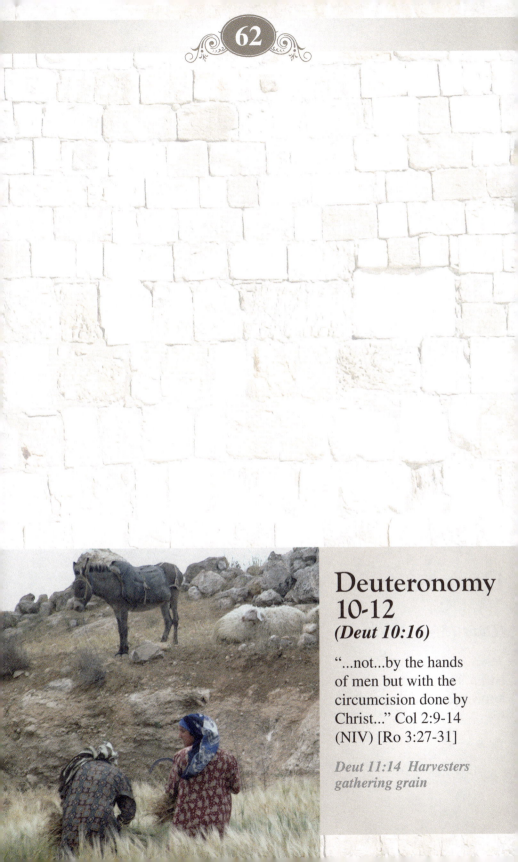

Deuteronomy 10-12
(Deut 10:16)

"...not...by the hands of men but with the circumcision done by Christ..." Col 2:9-14 (NIV) [Ro 3:27-31]

Deut 11:14 Harvesters gathering grain

Deuteronomy 13-15
(Deut 13:4)

Jesus answered: " 'My sheep listen to my voice; I know them and they follow me.' " Jn 10:27-30 (NLT)

*Deut 14:18
Hoopoe near Jerusalem*

Deuteronomy 16-17
(Deut 16:2)

"...the Galileans...took Him to their hearts eagerly, for they had seen everything that He did in Jerusalem during the feast..."
Jn 4:45 (AMP)

Deut 16:2 "...the place where the Lord will choose..." Jerusalem, an olive garden

Deuteronomy 18-20
(Deut 18:15)

" 'This is truly the Prophet who is to come into the world.' "
Jn 6:5, 9-14 (NASB)

Deut 19:14 Donkey in front of stone landmark

Deuteronomy 21-24
(Deut 21:6, 7)

"...Pilate...washed his hands in the presence of the crowd..." Mt 27:24 (AMP)

Deut 22:1, 2 "...you shall bring the animal to your house..."

Deuteronomy 25-28
(Deut 26:10)

"But now Christ has been raised from the dead, the first fruits of those who are asleep." 1Co 15:20 (NASB)

Deut 26:9 Bee at native Hollyhock flower

Deuteronomy 29-31
(Deut 30:6)

"...and in Him you were also circumcised with a circumcision made without hands..."
Col 2:11 (NASB)

Deuteronomy 32-34
(Deut 32:4)

"...they drank from the spiritual rock...and that rock was Christ."
1Co 10:1-4 (NLT)
[Num 20:1-8; Ps 78:15, 16; Jn 4:7-14; Jn 7:2, 37, 38]

Joshua 1-3
(Josh 1:5)

Jesus said to his disciples:
" '...I am with you always, even to the end of the age.' "
Mt 28:20 (NLT)
[Heb 13:5]

71

Joshua 4-6
(Josh 5:13-15)

"When I saw Him, I fell at His feet..."
Rv 1:1, 2, 12-17 (AMP)
[Is 44:6]

Josh 5:12 Sycamore tree

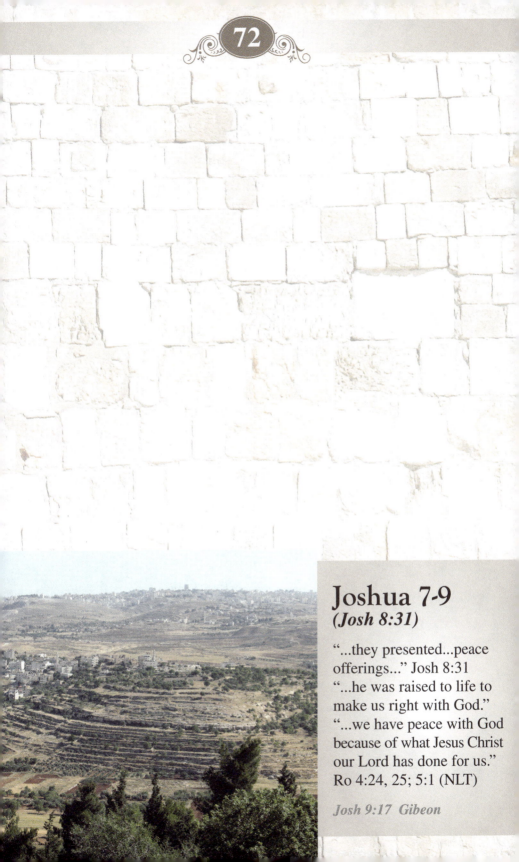

Joshua 7-9
(Josh 8:31)

"...they presented...peace offerings..." Josh 8:31
"...he was raised to life to make us right with God."
"...we have peace with God because of what Jesus Christ our Lord has done for us."
Ro 4:24, 25; 5:1 (NLT)

Josh 9:17 Gibeon

Joshua 10-12
(Josh 10:5)

"The kings of the earth took their stand... against the Lord and against His Anointed..."
Ac 4:26 (AMP)
[Ac 4:25-30; Ps 2:1, 2]

Joshua 13-16
(Josh 15:19)

" 'If you knew...who says to you, 'Give Me a drink,' you would have asked Him, and He would have given you living water.' "
Jn 4:7-14 (NASB)

Josh 15:1 Rufous Bush Robin, Wilderness of Zin

Joshua 17-19
(Josh 17:4)

"...we have been born again..." "...into an inheritance which is beyond the reach of change... reserved in heaven for you," "Who are being guarded... by God's power through [your] faith..."
1Pe 1:3-5 (AMP)

Josh 18:12 Carrying firewood in Jericho

Joshua 20-22
(Josh 22:4)

Jesus said: " 'Come to Me, all who are weary and heavy-laden, and I will give you rest.' " Mt 11:28 (NASB)

Josh 21:27 Goldfinches in the Golan region

Joshua 23-24
(Josh 24:10; Num 24:17)

" 'Where is the newborn king of the Jews? We saw his star as it rose, and we have come to worship him.' "
Mt 2:1, 2, 9-12 (NLT)

Josh 24:13 Young olive trees in spring

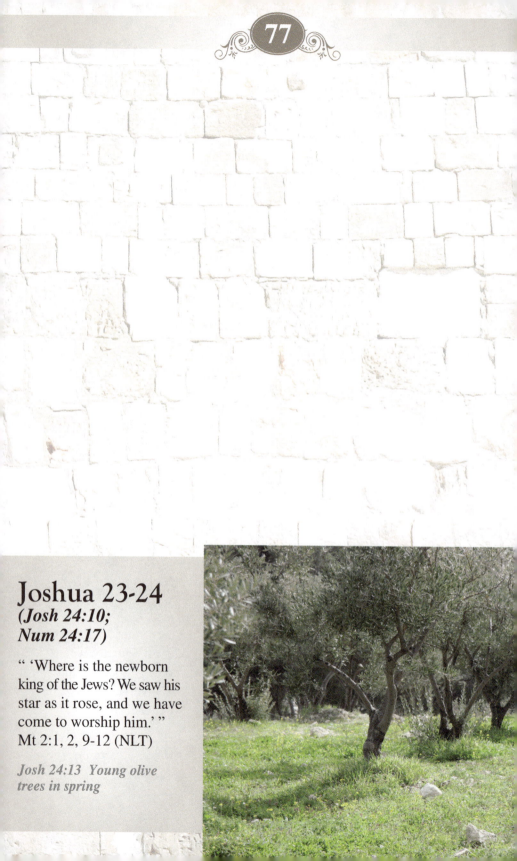

Judges 1-4
(Jg 2:7)

"Because you have seen Me, Thomas, do you now believe...? Blessed...are those who have never seen Me and yet have believed..." Jn 20:29 (AMP)

Jg 1:16 Tents near Arad

Judges 5-7
(Jg 6:8)

" 'The Spirit of the Lord is upon me...' '...He has sent me to proclaim that captives will be released...' "
Lk 4:14-21 (NLT)

Jg 6:2 Caves in the Hill country of Ephraim

Judges 8-12
(Jg 9:4-20)

Jesus said: "...for figs are not gathered from thorns nor is a cluster of grapes picked from a bramble bush..." Lk 6:44, 45 (AMP)

Jg 10:4 Young donkey

Judges 13-16
(Jg 13:8)

Jesus is Counselor and Teacher: "...His name shall be called Wonderful Counselor..." Is 9:6 "...we...are certain that You have come from God [as] a Teacher..." Jn 3:1, 2 (AMP)

Jg 14:8 Bee in flight

Judges 17-19
(Jg 17:6)

"...for us there is but one God..." 1Co 8:6
"...the Word was God... apart from Him nothing came into being that has come into being."
Jn 1:1-3 (NASB)

Judges 20-21
(Jg 21:25)

Jesus said: "But blessed ...are your eyes because they do see..." "...many prophets and righteous men...yearned to see what you see..."
Mt 13:14-17 (AMP)
[Is 6:9, 10]

Ruth 1-4
(Ruth 4:22)

"...by Ruth, and Obed the father of Jesse. Jesse was the father of David the king."
" '...Joseph, son of David...' "
"And Joseph...did as the angel of the Lord commanded him..."
Mt 1:5, 6, 20-25 (NASB)

Ruth 2:2 Young woman harvesting

85

1 Samuel 1-5
(1Sa 1:15)

Jesus said: "...for such people the Father seeks to be His worshipers." Jn 4:21-26 (NASB)

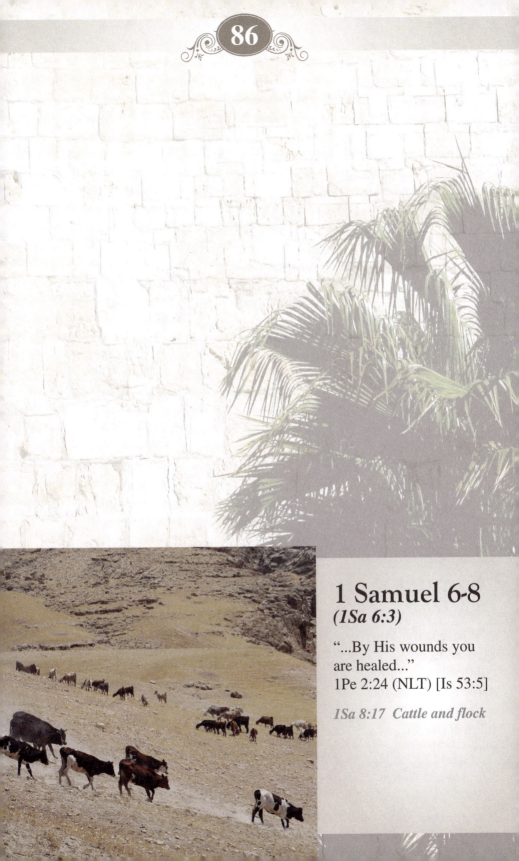

1 Samuel 6-8
(1Sa 6:3)

"...By His wounds you are healed..."
1Pe 2:24 (NLT) [Is 53:5]

1Sa 8:17 Cattle and flock

1 Samuel 9-11
(1Sa 9:17)

"...'Where is the Messiah supposed to be born?'"
" 'In Bethlehem, in Judea...' "
" 'For this is what the prophet wrote...' "
Mt 2:4-6 (NLT)
[Micah 5:2]

1Sa 9:3 Baby donkey and mother

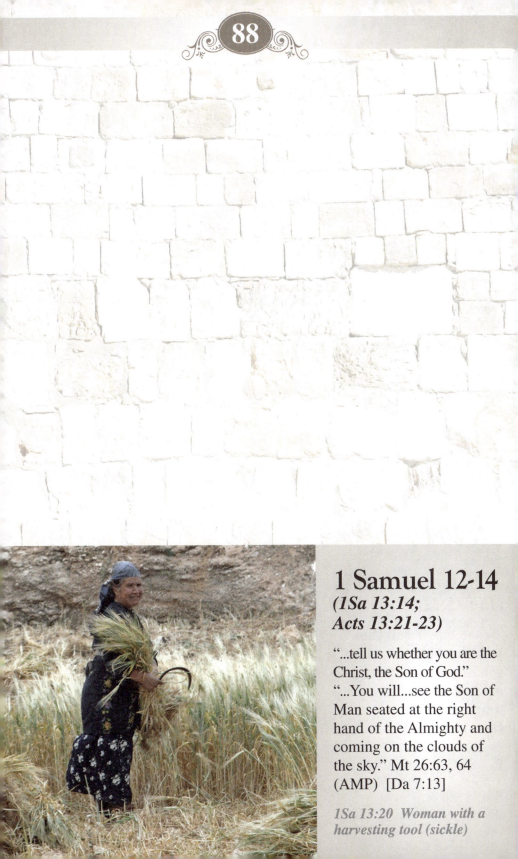

1 Samuel 12-14
(1Sa 13:14; Acts 13:21-23)

"...tell us whether you are the Christ, the Son of God." "...You will...see the Son of Man seated at the right hand of the Almighty and coming on the clouds of the sky." Mt 26:63, 64 (AMP) [Da 7:13]

1Sa 13:20 Woman with a harvesting tool (sickle)

1 Samuel 15-18
(1Sa 15:22)

Jesus said: "I will show you what he is like who comes to me and hears my words and puts them into practice..."
Lk 6:46-48 (NIV)
[*A prayer of David:* Ps 86:11, 12]

*1Sa 16:18, 19
Bethlehem sheep*

1 Samuel 19-21
(1Sa 21:5)

Jesus says of Himself:
"...These are the words of him who is holy and true, who holds the key of David."
Rv 3:7 (NIV)

1 Samuel 22-24
(1Sa 23:16)

"For whoever does the will of My Father in heaven is My brother, and sister and mother!"
Mt 12:48-50 (AMP)

1Sa 22:3 Ibex at Ein Gedi: across the Dead Sea is Moab where David's grandmother, Ruth, is from

1 Samuel 25-28
(1Sa 26:11)

Jesus said: "But I say to you who hear...do good to those who hate you, bless those who curse you, pray for those who mistreat you." Lk 6:27, 28 (NASB)

1Sa 24:1 Ibex mother and baby in the wilderness of Engedi (also known as Ein Gedi)

93

1 Samuel 29-31
(1Sa 30:8)

" 'I do exactly as the Father commanded me...' "
Jn 14:31 (NASB)

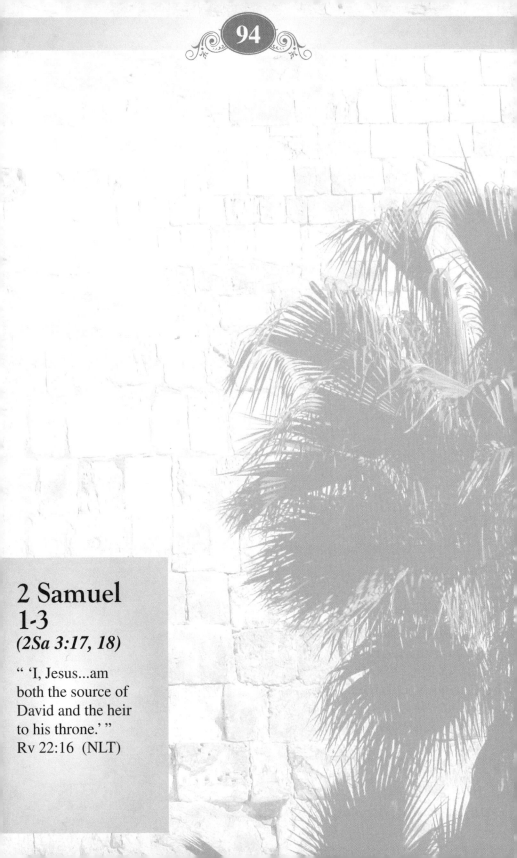

2 Samuel 1-3
(2Sa 3:17, 18)

" 'I, Jesus...am both the source of David and the heir to his throne.' "
Rv 22:16 (NLT)

2 Samuel 4-7
(2Sa 7:16)

"...he knew God had promised with an oath that one of David's own descendants would sit on his throne. David was... speaking of the Messiah's resurrection."
Ac 2:29-36 (NLT)
[Ps 110:1]

2Sa 5:5 Jerusalem

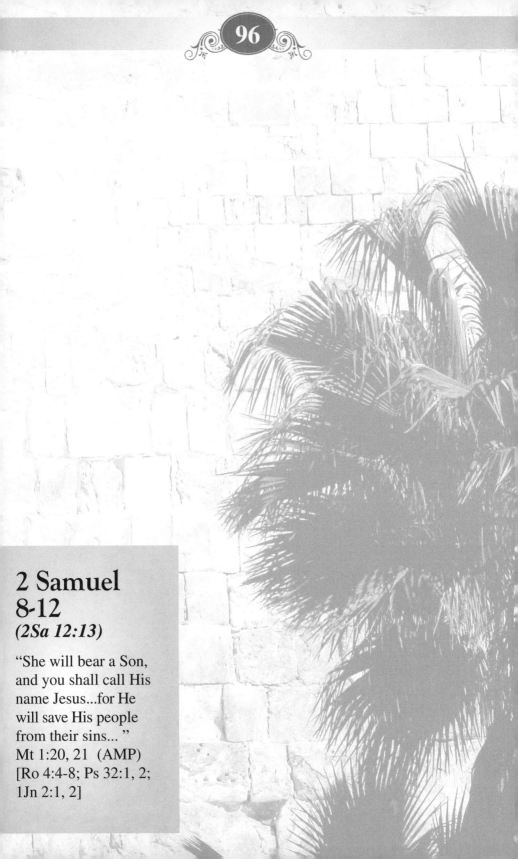

2 Samuel 8-12
(2Sa 12:13)

"She will bear a Son, and you shall call His name Jesus...for He will save His people from their sins..."
Mt 1:20, 21 (AMP)
[Ro 4:4-8; Ps 32:1, 2; 1Jn 2:1, 2]

2 Samuel 13-16
(2Sa 16:5-12)

"Do not repay anyone evil for evil..." Ro 12:17-21
Jesus said: " '...love your enemies, do good...' " Lk 6:27, 35 (NIV)

2Sa 15:30 Dawn over Jordan and the Dead Sea, viewed from the Mount of Olives

2 Samuel 17-18
(2Sa 18:28)

"...Jesus Christ...will be shown forth in His own proper time by the blessed, only Sovereign (Ruler), the King of kings and the Lord of lords..."
1Ti 6:14, 15 (AMP)

2Sa 17:28 Beans, lentils and seeds in the Old City Jerusalem market

2 Samuel 19-21
(2Sa 19:8)

"...the Lord God will give to Him the throne of His forefather David." "...and of His reign there will be no end." Lk 1:31-35 (AMP) [Is 9:7; Da 2:44]

2Sa 19:43 Ibex contending, "back and forth" (NLT), at Ein Gedi

2 Samuel 22-24
(2Sa 22:29)

Jesus said: " 'I am the Light of the world...' "
Jn 8:12; 12:44-46
2Sa 23:5
" '...to remember His holy covenant...' "
Lk 1:68-72 (NASB)
[Ac 4:8-12; Ps 118:22]

1 Kings 1-3
(1Ki 3:5)

" 'Until now you have asked for nothing in My name; ask and you shall receive, so that your joy may be made full.' "
Jn 16:23, 24   (NASB)

1Ki 2:10 City of David south of the Temple Mount

Psalms 1-4
(Ps 2:2)

" 'The kings of the earth prepared for battle; the rulers gathered together against the LORD and against his Messiah.' "
Ac 4:24-30 (NLT)
[Ac 13:32-38; Ps 2:7]

Ps 1:3 Trees growing in spring at the banks of the stream of Caesarea Philippi

103

Psalms 5-7
(Ps 5:7)

"Because of your unfailing love..." Ps 5:7
"...not that we loved God, but that he loved us..."
"...we have seen with our own eyes...the Father sent his Son to be the Savior of the world."
1Jn 4:9, 10, 13, 14 (NLT)

104

Psalms 8-11
(Ps 8:2)

"...the chief priests and the scribes saw...the youths and the maidens crying out...Hosanna...to the Son of David!..." "...have you never read, Out of the mouth of babes...You have made...perfect praise?" Mt 21:14-16 (AMP)

Psalms 12-16
(Ps 16:10)

"We believe and know that you are the Holy One of God." Jn 6:67-69 (NIV)
[Ac 13:32-35; Ps 2:7; Is 55:3]

Ps 16:6 Jerusalem

Psalms 17-20
(Ps 19:1)

"For he rescued us...and transferred us to the kingdom of His beloved Son..." "He is the image of the invisible God..." "For by Him all things were created...all things have been created through Him and for Him."
Col 1:13-17 (NASB)

Ps 19:5 Wedding in Jerusalem

Psalms 21-22
(Ps 22:27-31)

"...taking the form of a bond-servant, and being made in the likeness of men." "...at the name of Jesus EVERY KNEE WILL BOW..."
Php 2:7-11 (NASB)
[Heb 9:11-15, 24-26]

Psalms 23-26
(Ps 25:14)

"...(the Spirit) will take the things that are Mine and will reveal...it to you." Jn 16:12-15 (AMP)

Ps 23:2 Lamb lying in green pasture

Psalms 27-31
(Ps 27:8)

"For God Who said, Let light shine out of darkness, has shone in our hearts so as [to beam forth] the... glory of God in the face of Jesus Christ (the Messiah)."
2Co 4:6 (AMP)

Ps 27:5 Nubian Ibex high up above Wadi Arugot at Ein Gedi

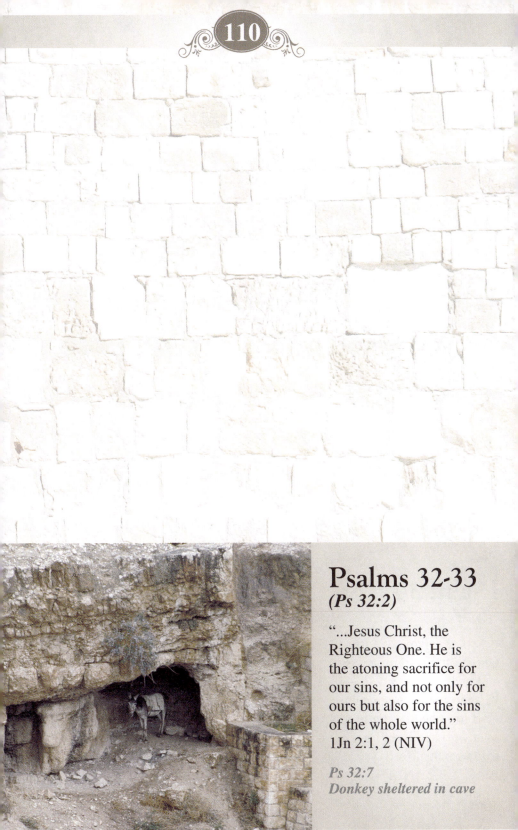

Psalms 32-33
(Ps 32:2)

"...Jesus Christ, the Righteous One. He is the atoning sacrifice for our sins, and not only for ours but also for the sins of the whole world."
1Jn 2:1, 2 (NIV)

Ps 32:7
Donkey sheltered in cave

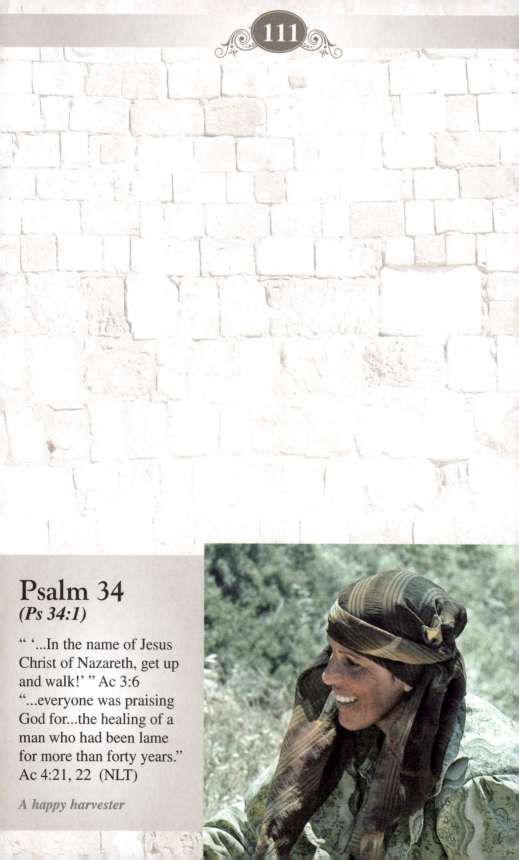

Psalm 34
(Ps 34:1)

" '...In the name of Jesus Christ of Nazareth, get up and walk!' " Ac 3:6
"...everyone was praising God for...the healing of a man who had been lame for more than forty years." Ac 4:21, 22 (NLT)

A happy harvester

Psalms 35-37
(Ps 35:19)

"...They hated Me without a cause..." "But when the Comforter...comes, Whom I will send to you from the Father...He [Himself] will testify regarding Me."
Jn 15:23-27 (AMP)

Ps 36:7 Chukar chicks near Bethlehem

Psalms 38-40
(Ps 40:6-8)

"Hence, when He [Christ] entered into the world, He said..."
"...Behold, here I am ...to do Your will..."
"...we have been... (...sanctified) through ...(the Anointed One)."
Heb 10:3-10 (AMP)

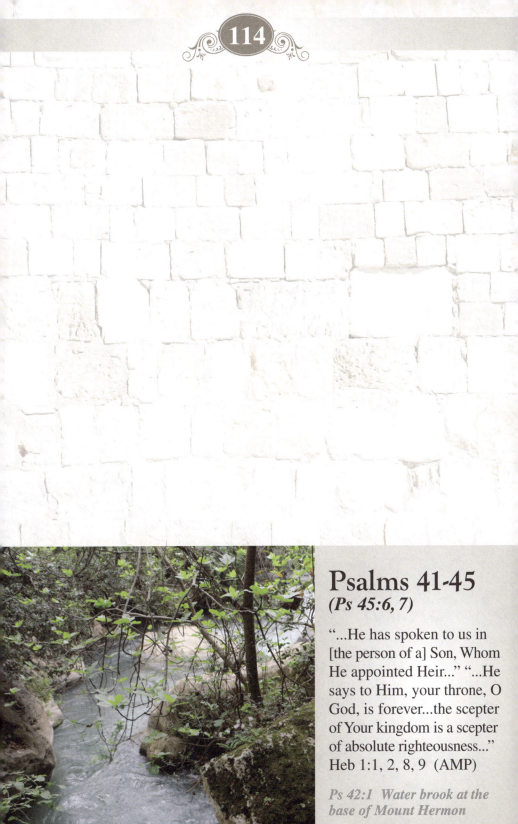

Psalms 41-45
(Ps 45:6, 7)

"...He has spoken to us in [the person of a] Son, Whom He appointed Heir..." "...He says to Him, your throne, O God, is forever...the scepter of Your kingdom is a scepter of absolute righteousness..." Heb 1:1, 2, 8, 9 (AMP)

Ps 42:1 Water brook at the base of Mount Hermon

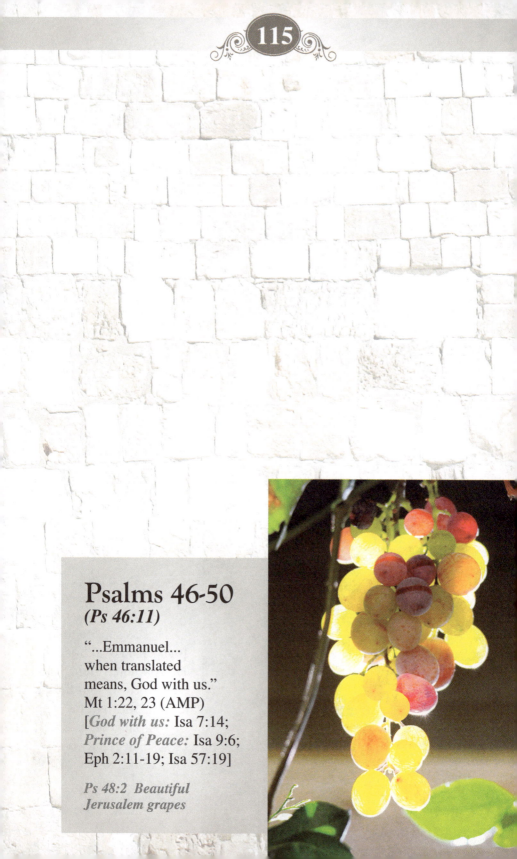

Psalms 46-50
(Ps 46:11)

"...Emmanuel...
when translated
means, God with us."
Mt 1:22, 23 (AMP)
[*God with us:* Isa 7:14;
Prince of Peace: Isa 9:6;
Eph 2:11-19; Isa 57:19]

*Ps 48:2 Beautiful
Jerusalem grapes*

Psalms 51-55
(Ps 51:7)

"And He stretched out His hand and touched him, saying 'I am willing; be cleansed.'"
Lk 5:12, 13 (NASB)
[1Jn 1:7]

Ps 55:6 Dove in Jerusalem

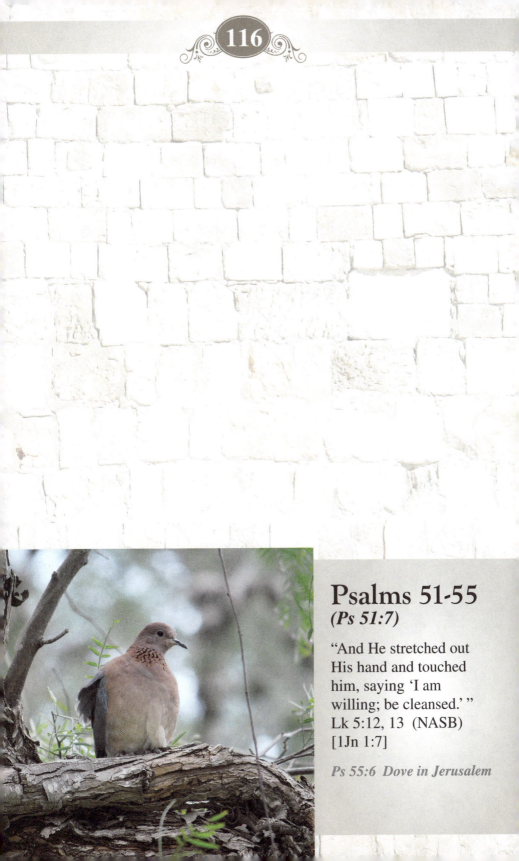

Psalms 56-60
(Ps 57:1)

"How often I wanted to gather your children together, the way a hen gathers her chicks under her wings..."
Mt 23:1, 10, 37 (NASB)
[Mt 2:4-6; Micah 5:2; Ge 49:10]

Psalms 61-65
(Ps 65:7a)

"When Jesus woke up, he rebuked the waves, 'Silence! Be Still!' "
Mk 4:35-41 (NLT)

Sea of Galilee

Psalms 66-68
(Ps 66:5)

"We all know that God has sent you to teach us. Your miraculous signs are evidence that God is with you." Jn 3:1, 2 (NLT)

Ps 67:6 Harvester

Psalms 69-71
(Ps 69:9)

"...Take these things away...! Make not My Father's house a house of merchandise (a market place, a sales shop)!"
Jn 2:16, 17 (AMP)

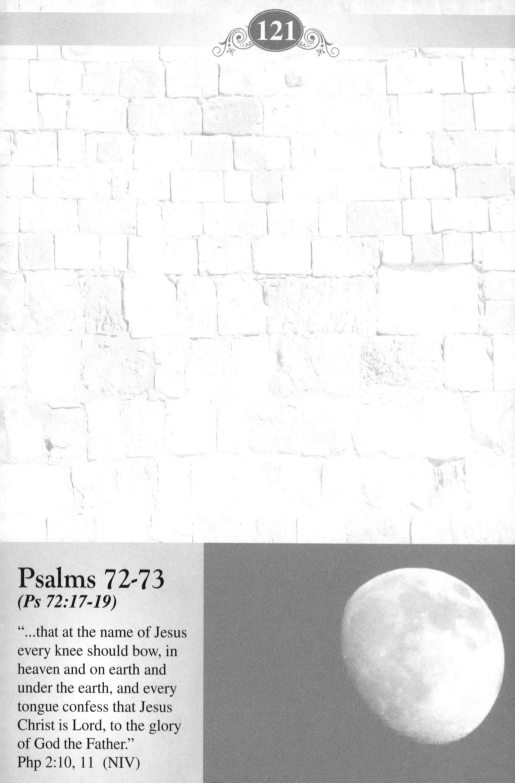

Psalms 72-73
(Ps 72:17-19)

"...that at the name of Jesus every knee should bow, in heaven and on earth and under the earth, and every tongue confess that Jesus Christ is Lord, to the glory of God the Father."
Php 2:10, 11 (NIV)

Ps 72:5
Moon over Jerusalem

Psalms 74-77
(Ps 77:20)

Jesus speaks: "I am the Good Shepherd; and I know and recognize My own..." Jn 10:14-16 (AMP) [Eze 34:23]

Shepherd walking his flock to sheepfold

Psalms 78-79
(Ps 78:24)

"Jesus replied, I am the Bread of Life. He who comes to Me will never be hungry..." Jn 6:30-35 (AMP) [Jn 6:47-51; Ex 16:14, 15, 35]

Num 33:36 Wilderness of Zin region

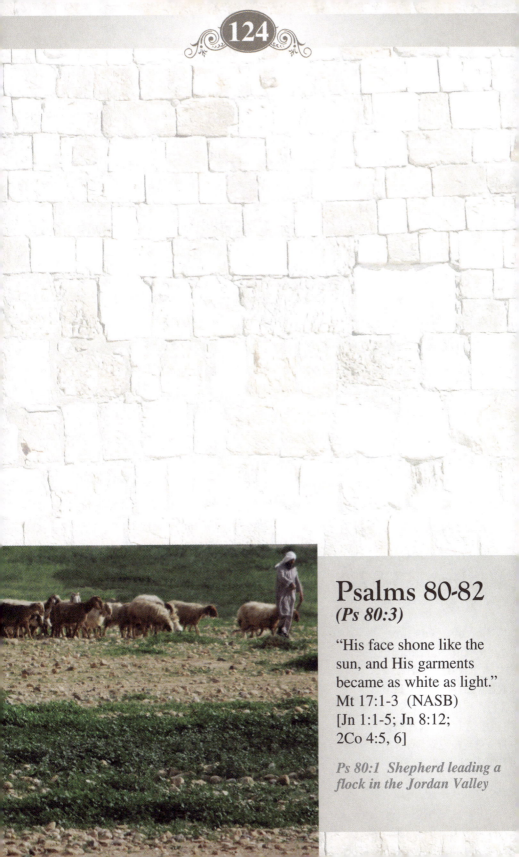

Psalms 80-82
(Ps 80:3)

"His face shone like the sun, and His garments became as white as light." Mt 17:1-3 (NASB)
[Jn 1:1-5; Jn 8:12; 2Co 4:5, 6]

Ps 80:1 Shepherd leading a flock in the Jordan Valley

Psalms 83-87
(Ps 86:9)

" 'For my eyes have seen your salvation...' "
" 'A LIGHT OF REVELATION TO THE GENTILES...' "
Lk 2:25-32 (NASB)
[Lk 1:26, 27, 30-35; Is 42:6]

Ps 84:3 Swallow in the Galilee region

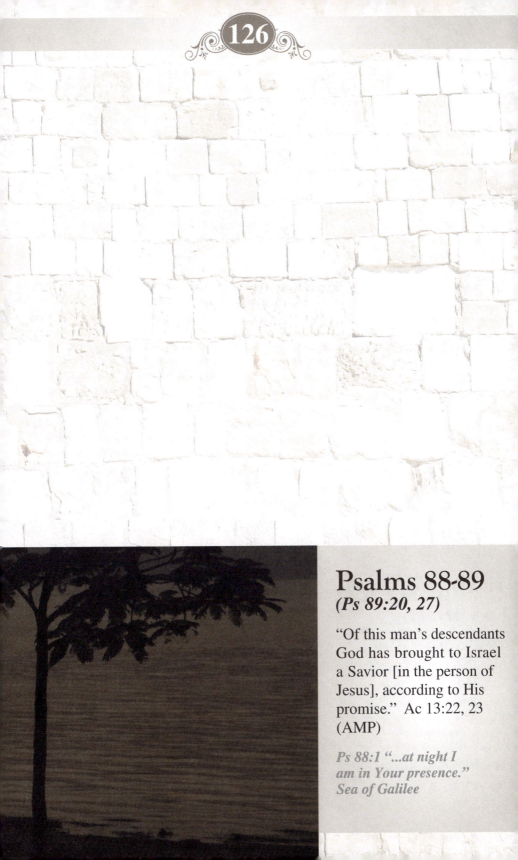

Psalms 88-89
(Ps 89:20, 27)

"Of this man's descendants God has brought to Israel a Savior [in the person of Jesus], according to His promise." Ac 13:22, 23 (AMP)

Ps 88:1 "...at night I am in Your presence." Sea of Galilee

Psalms 90-92
(Ps 91:11, 12)

"And Jesus replied to him...You shall not tempt (try, test exceedingly) the Lord your God."
Lk 4:9-12 (AMP)
[Deut 6:16; Ex 17:7]

Ps 92:12 Date palm tree near Jericho

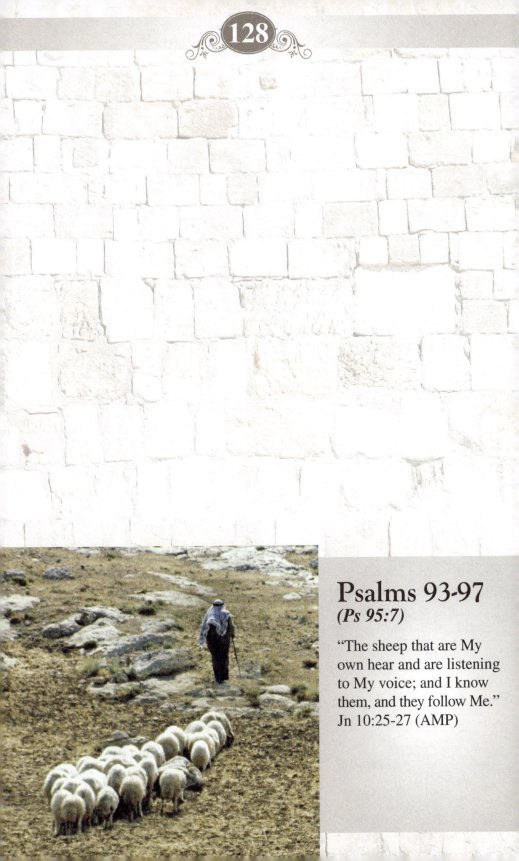

Psalms 93-97
(Ps 95:7)

"The sheep that are My own hear and are listening to My voice; and I know them, and they follow Me."
Jn 10:25-27 (AMP)

Psalms 98-102
(Ps 102:27)

"But you remain the same, and your years will never end."
Heb 1:1-3, 10-12 (NIV)
[Rv 1:1, 2; 5:13]

*Ps 100:3
Sheep in Galilee pasture*

Psalm 103
(Ps 103:1-3)

"...and He laid His hands upon every one of them and cured them."
Lk 4:40 (AMP)

Ps 103:15 Spring flowers along the Jordan Valley

Psalms 104-105
(Ps 104:5)

"...He is the exact likeness of the unseen God [the visible representation of the invisible]..." "...all things were created and exist through Him..." Col 1:13-18 (AMP)

Ps 104:12 Sunbird nest

Psalm 106
(Ps 106:44, 45)

"Seeing the people, He felt compassion for them, because they were distressed and dispirited like sheep without a shepherd."
Mt 9:35, 36 (NASB)

Psalm 107
(Ps 107:14, 15)

" '...the Sunrise from on high will visit us, TO SHINE UPON THOSE WHO SIT IN DARKNESS AND THE SHADOW OF DEATH...' "
Lk 1:78,79 (NASB)
[Is 9:2, 6, 7; Mt 4:16]

Ps 107:38 Cattle in Manasseh-Jordan Valley region

Psalms 108-109
(Ps 109:25)

" 'But I will send you the Advocate...' 'He will come to you from the Father and will testify all about me.' "
Jn 15:26 (NLT)
[Mt 27:39, 40; 28:5-7]

Ps 108:10 Petra, in the Edom region

Psalms 110-114
(Ps 110:1)

"...the champion who initiates and perfects our faith..." "Now he is seated in the place of honor..." Heb 12:1, 2 (NLT) [Rv 21:3, 4]

Ps 114:8 Flint (AMP) (NASB) rock behind Nubian Ibex at Ein Avdat, Wilderness of Zin

Psalms 115-117
(Ps 115:1)

"Jesus said to him, I am the Way and the Truth and the Life..."
Jn 14:6 (AMP)

137

Psalm 118
(Ps 118:26)

"...They shouted, 'Praise God! Blessings on the one who comes in the name of the LORD!'..."
Jn 12:12, 13 (NLT)

Psalm 119
(Ps 119:24)

"Whoever receives His testimony has set his seal of approval to this: God is true..." Jn 3:33-35 (AMP) [Dan 7:13, 14]

Ps 119:103 Honeybee

Psalms 120-130
(Ps 122:1-5)

"...with my [own] eyes I have seen Your Salvation... Which You have ordained and prepared before (in the presence of) all peoples..."
Lk 2:25-32 (AMP)

Ps 121:1 Jerusalem hillside

Psalms 131-134
(Ps 132:11)

"...because he was a prophet and knew that GOD HAD SWORN TO HIM WITH AN OATH TO SEAT one OF HIS DESCENDANTS ON HIS THRONE..."
Ac 2:5-11, 29-36 (NASB)
[Ps 16:10; 110:1]

Ps 131:2

Psalms 135-139
(Ps 139:4)

"...all things are open and laid bare to the eyes of him with whom we have to do." Heb 4:12-16 (NASB)

Ps 136:25 Harvesting grain

Psalms 140-143
(Ps 143:8)

"...Lord, to whom would we go? You have the words that give eternal life. We believe, and we know you are the Holy One of God."
Jn 6:68, 69 (NLT)

Ps 143:6 Waterfall at Ein Gedi

143

Psalms 144-145
(Ps 145:13)

"Now to the King of eternity, incorruptible and immortal, invisible, the only God, be honor and glory forever..."
1Ti 1:15-17 (AMP)

Ps 144:13 Sheep on flowering hillside between Jerusalem and Jericho

Psalm 146
(Ps 146:8)

"...So I went and washed, and now I can see!"
Jn 9:1-11   (NLT)
[Lk 9:9-11]

Ps 146:6 "...the sea and everything in them..."
Emperor Angelfish, Gulf of Aqaba and Eilat

Psalm 147
(Ps 147:3)

"He has sent me to proclaim freedom for the prisoners...to release the oppressed."
Lk 4:14-21 (NIV)
[Is 61:1, 2]

Ps 147:14 Taking the wheat to be winnowed

146

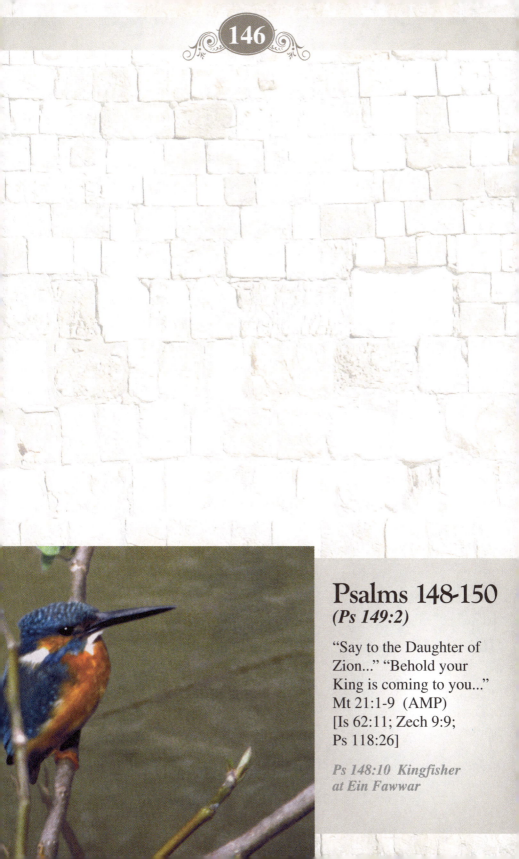

Psalms 148-150
(Ps 149:2)

"Say to the Daughter of Zion..." "Behold your King is coming to you..." Mt 21:1-9 (AMP) [Is 62:11; Zech 9:9; Ps 118:26]

Ps 148:10 Kingfisher at Ein Fawwar

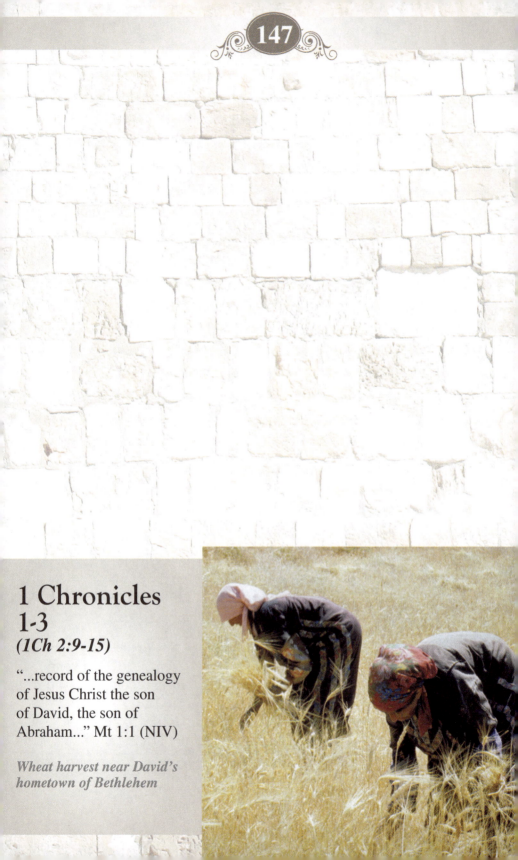

1 Chronicles 1-3
(1Ch 2:9-15)

"...record of the genealogy of Jesus Christ the son of David, the son of Abraham..." Mt 1:1 (NIV)

Wheat harvest near David's hometown of Bethlehem

1 Chronicles 4-6
(1Ch 5:2)

" '...Bethlehem, in the land of Judah...' '...out of you will come a ruler who will be the shepherd of my people Israel.' "
Mt 2:6 (NIV) [Micah 5:2]

1Ch 6:32 Tabernacle reconstruction

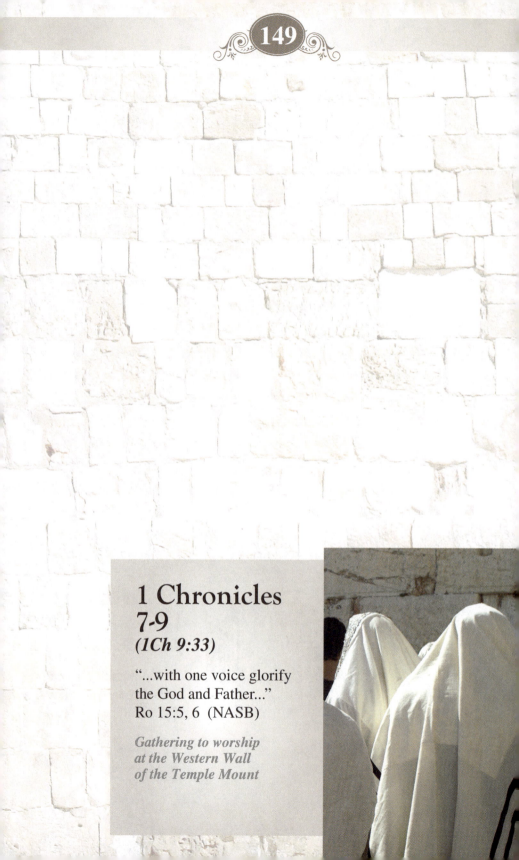

1 Chronicles 7-9
(1Ch 9:33)

"...with one voice glorify the God and Father..." Ro 15:5, 6 (NASB)

Gathering to worship at the Western Wall of the Temple Mount

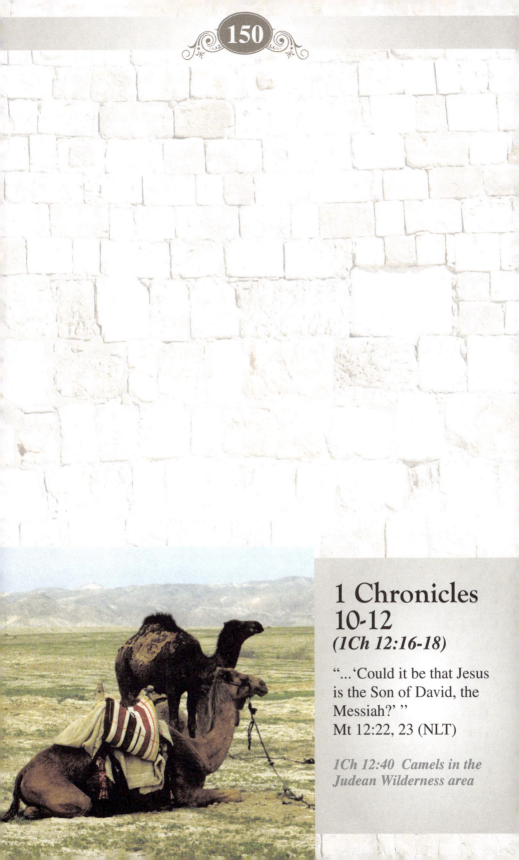

1 Chronicles 10-12
(1Ch 12:16-18)

"...'Could it be that Jesus is the Son of David, the Messiah?'"
Mt 12:22, 23 (NLT)

1Ch 12:40 Camels in the Judean Wilderness area

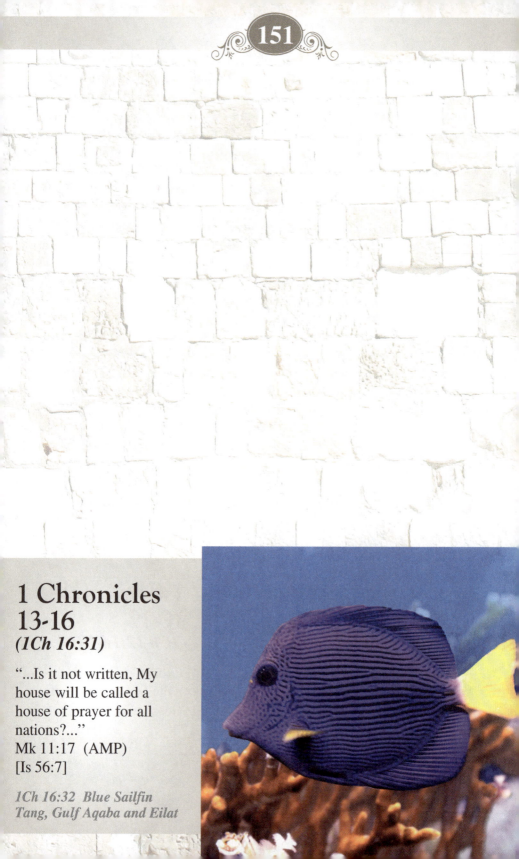

1 Chronicles 13-16
(1Ch 16:31)

"...Is it not written, My house will be called a house of prayer for all nations?..."
Mk 11:17 (AMP)
[Is 56:7]

1Ch 16:32 Blue Sailfin Tang, Gulf Aqaba and Eilat

1 Chronicles 17-20
(1Ch 17:14)

"And he will reign over Israel forever; his Kingdom will never end."
Lk 1:32, 33 (NLT)
[Is 9:7]

1Ch 17:7 Sheep feeding on the winter grasses

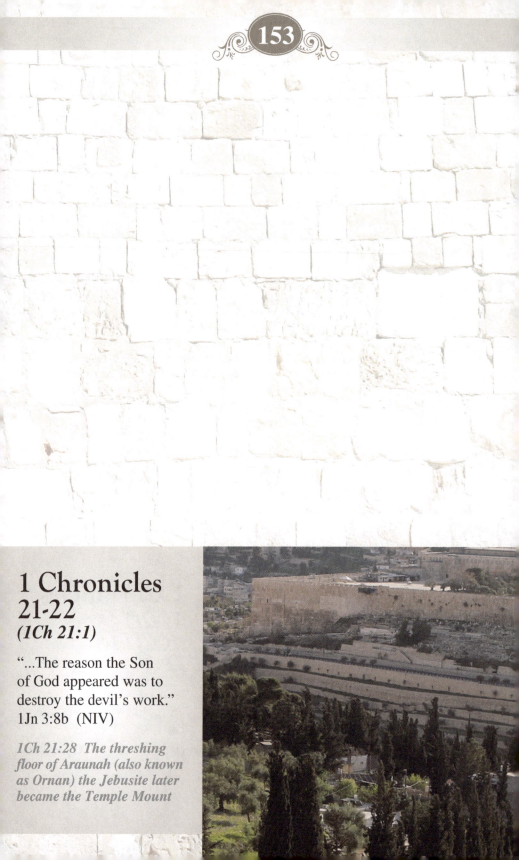

1 Chronicles 21-22
(1Ch 21:1)

"...The reason the Son of God appeared was to destroy the devil's work."
1Jn 3:8b (NIV)

1Ch 21:28 The threshing floor of Araunah (also known as Ornan) the Jebusite later became the Temple Mount

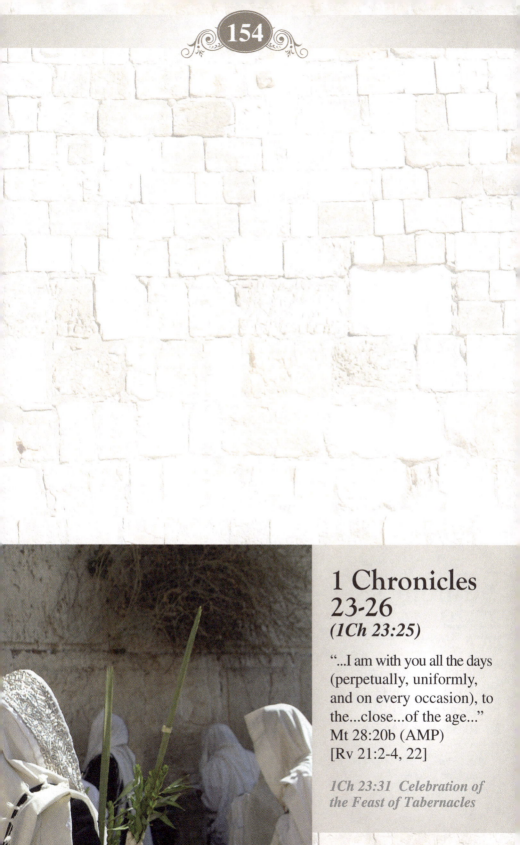

1 Chronicles 23-26
(1Ch 23:25)

"...I am with you all the days (perpetually, uniformly, and on every occasion), to the...close...of the age..."
Mt 28:20b (AMP)
[Rv 21:2-4, 22]

1Ch 23:31 Celebration of the Feast of Tabernacles

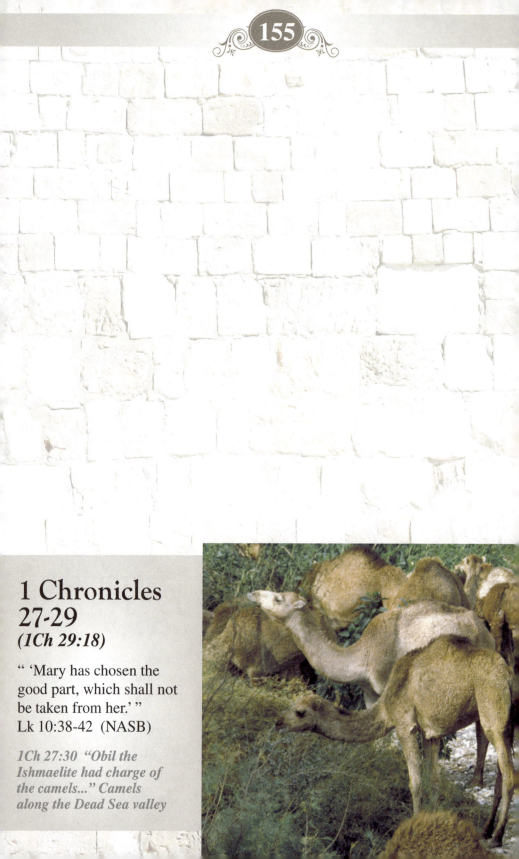

1 Chronicles 27-29
(1Ch 29:18)

" 'Mary has chosen the good part, which shall not be taken from her.' "
Lk 10:38-42 (NASB)

1Ch 27:30 "Obil the Ishmaelite had charge of the camels..." Camels along the Dead Sea valley

2 Chronicles 1-3
(2Ch 2:5, 6)

"Jesus answered them, Destroy (undo) this temple, and in three days I will raise it up again." Jn 2:19 (AMP) [Rv 21:22]

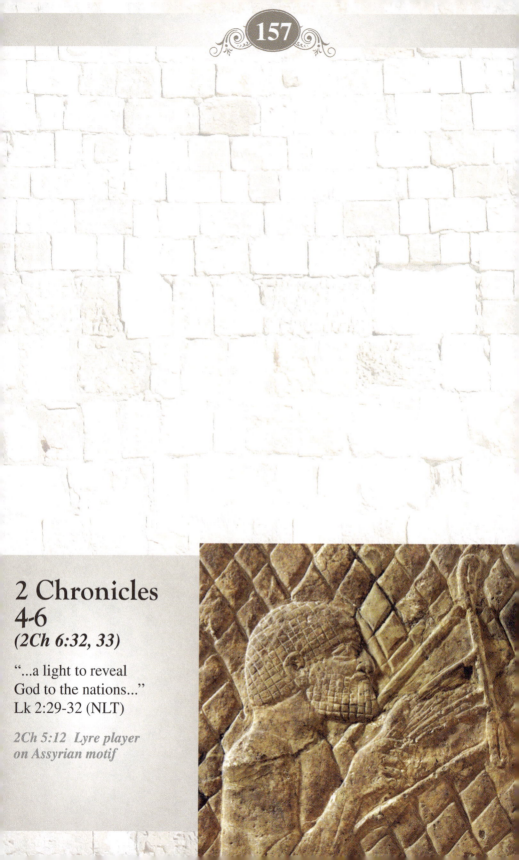

2 Chronicles 4-6
(2Ch 6:32, 33)

"...a light to reveal God to the nations..."
Lk 2:29-32 (NLT)

2Ch 5:12 Lyre player on Assyrian motif

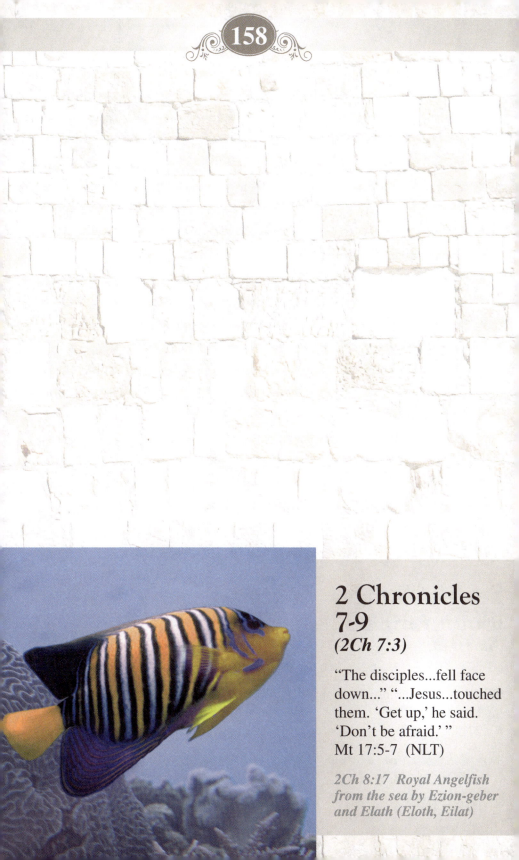

2 Chronicles 7-9
(2Ch 7:3)

"The disciples...fell face down..." "...Jesus...touched them. 'Get up,' he said. 'Don't be afraid.'"
Mt 17:5-7 (NLT)

2Ch 8:17 Royal Angelfish from the sea by Ezion-geber and Elath (Eloth, Eilat)

Song of Songs (Solomon) 1-3
(SS 3:11b)

"...Come with me! I will show you the bride, the Lamb's wife."
Rv 21:9b (AMP)

King Solomon's Crown flower, also known as Cyclamen

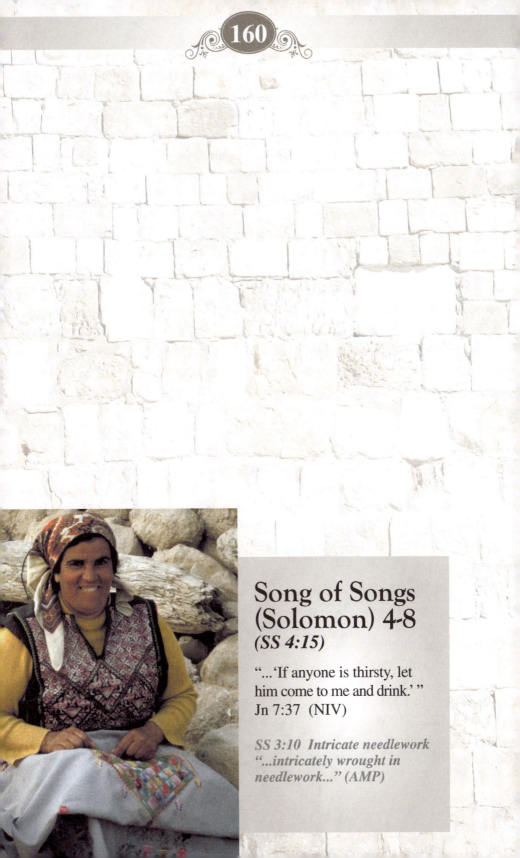

Song of Songs (Solomon) 4-8
(SS 4:15)

"...'If anyone is thirsty, let him come to me and drink.'"
Jn 7:37 (NIV)

SS 3:10 Intricate needlework
"...intricately wrought in needlework..." (AMP)

Proverbs 1-3
(Pr 3:19)

"Through him all things were made; without him nothing was made that has been made." Jn 1:1-3 (NIV) [Col 2:2, 3]

SS 8:14 Mountain Gazelle

Proverbs 4-7
(Pr 4:18)

"Let your light shine before men, that they may see...and praise your Father in heaven." Mt 4:23-25; 5:1, 2, 14-16 (NIV)

Pr 4:18 Sunrise at Jericho

Proverbs 8-11
(Pr 8:1, 29, 30)

"...that you may be filled with the full (deep and clear) knowledge of His will in all spiritual wisdom..."
Col 1:5-9 (AMP)

Pr 11:26 Grain bundle

Proverbs 12-15
(Pr 14:27)

"...the water that I will give him shall become a spring of water welling up...within him unto...eternal life."
Jn 4:6-10, 13, 14 (AMP)

Pr 14:21 A cup of hospitality

Proverbs 16-19
(Pr 16:2)

"But Jesus would not entrust himself to them, for he knew all men..."
Jn 2:24, 25 (NIV)
[Pr 19:21; Ac 5:29-35, 38, 39]

Pr 16:7

Proverbs 20-21
(Pr 20:22)

"For the Son of Man came to seek and to save that which was lost."
Lk 19:10 (AMP)

Pr 20:4 Plowing

Proverbs 22-24
(Pr 23:6, 7)

"...These people [constantly] honor Me with their lips, but their hearts hold off and are far distant from Me." Mk 7:1-23 (AMP) [Is 29:13]

Pr 23:10 Close-up of boundary marker

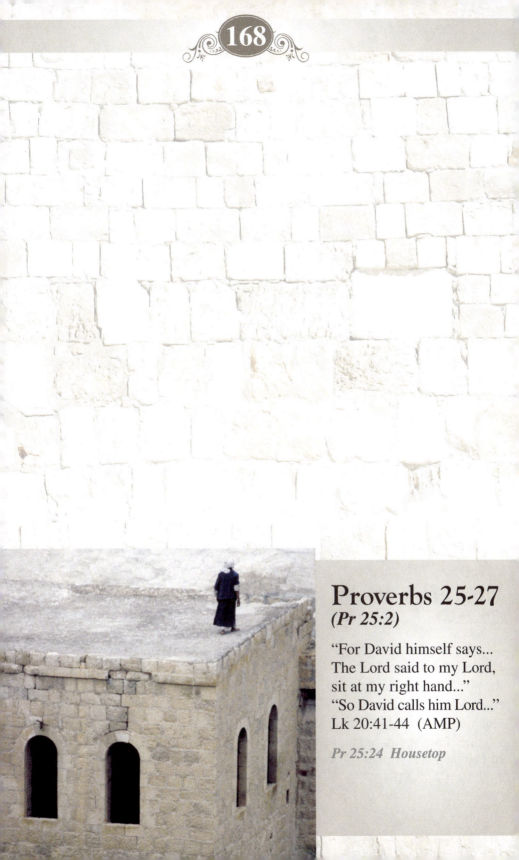

Proverbs 25-27
(Pr 25:2)

"For David himself says...
The Lord said to my Lord,
sit at my right hand..."
"So David calls him Lord..."
Lk 20:41-44 (AMP)

Pr 25:24 Housetop

Proverbs 28-29
(Pr 28:5)

"If any man desires to do His will...he will know (have the needed illumination to recognize...) whether the teaching is from God or whether I am speaking... of My own accord..."
Jn 7:16, 17 (AMP)

Pr 28:19 Cultivating

Proverbs 30-31
(Pr 30:4)

"No one has ever gone into heaven except the one who came from heaven – the Son of Man." Jn 3:13
"...Jesus the Son of God..." Heb 4:14-16 (NIV)

Pr 31:16 Carrying a grapevine basket

Ecclesiastes 1-6
(Ecc 2:25)

" '...I came that they may have life, and have it abundantly.' "
Jn 10:10 (NASB)

Ecc 4:9 Two women harvesting together

Ecclesiastes 7-12
(Ecc 12:13)

"... 'if anyone loves me, he will obey my teaching. My Father will love him, and we will come to him and make our home with him.'"
Jn 14:21-26 (NIV)

Ecc 11:4 Woman reaping her harvest

1 Kings 4-7
(1Ki 6:1)

"I tell you that one greater than the temple is here."
Mt 12:6 (NIV)

1Ki 4:28

1 Kings 8-9
(1Ki 8:41-43)

"Is it not written: 'My house will be called a house of prayer for all nations?' "
Mk 11:15-17 (NIV)
[Is 56:6-8; Rv 22:1, 2]

1 Kings 10-11
(1Ki 10:6, 7)

" 'The Queen of the South... came from the ends of the earth to hear the wisdom of Solomon; and behold, something greater than Solomon is here.' "
Mt 12:42 (NASB)

1Ki 10:22 Peacock at Hamat Gadar

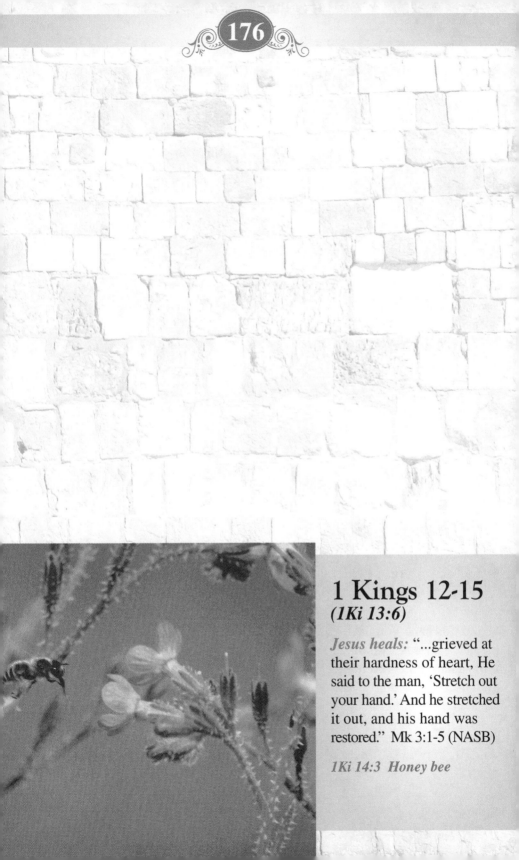

1 Kings 12-15
(1Ki 13:6)

Jesus heals: "...grieved at their hardness of heart, He said to the man, 'Stretch out your hand.' And he stretched it out, and his hand was restored." Mk 3:1-5 (NASB)

1Ki 14:3 Honey bee

1 Kings 16-18
(1Ki 18:37)

"Up to this time you have not asked a [single] thing in My Name [as presenting all that I AM]; but now ask and keep on asking..."
Jn 16:20-28 (AMP)

1Ki 17:4 Fan-tailed Ravens; residents of the Jordan Valley, Dead Sea area

1 Kings 19-22
(1Ki 21:4)

Jesus said: "...as for what fell among the thorns, these are [the people] who hear, but as they go on their way they are choked...with the ...cares and riches and pleasures of life..."
Lk 8:4-7, 14, 15 (AMP)

1Ki 19:4 White Broom blooming in spring

2 Chronicles 10-13
(2Ch 13:18)

" '...the Lion of the tribe of Judah, the Root of David, has triumphed...' "
Rv 5:5 (NIV)

2Ch 10:16 Tents

2 Chronicles 14-16
(2Ch 16:9a)

"...He is a rewarder of those who earnestly and diligently seek Him [out]."
Heb 11:6 (AMP)

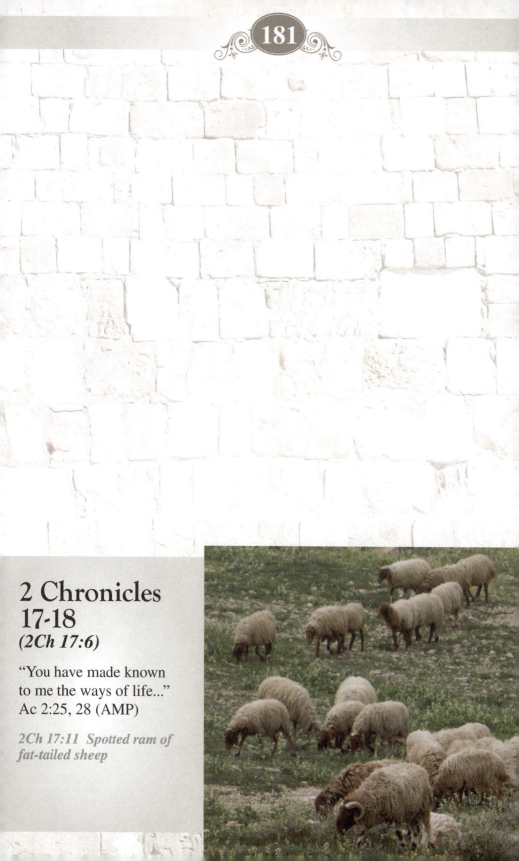

2 Chronicles 17-18
(2Ch 17:6)

"You have made known to me the ways of life..."
Ac 2:25, 28 (AMP)

2Ch 17:11 Spotted ram of fat-tailed sheep

2 Kings 1-3
(2Ki 1:3)

"And he will [himself] go before Him in the spirit and power of Elijah, to turn back the hearts of... the disobedient...to the wisdom of the upright..."
Lk 1:5, 8, 9, 11-17 (AMP)

2Ki 2:13, 14 The Jordan River near Jericho

2 Chronicles 19-21
(2Ch 20:6)

"...that at the name of Jesus every knee should bow, in heaven and on earth..."
Php 2:5-10 (NIV)
[Mt 28:18]

2Ch 20:2 Ibex at En Gedi (Ein Gedi)

2 Kings 4-6
(2Ki 5:6-14)

"Jesus reached out his hand and touched the man. 'I am willing,' he said. 'Be clean!' And immediately the leprosy left him."
Lk 5:13 (NIV)

2Ki 5:1; Lk 4:27 "Naaman the Syrian" Syrian Pear tree near Bethlehem

2 Kings 7-10
(2Ki 8:5)

"And the man [who was] dead sat up and began to speak. And [Jesus] gave him [back] to his mother."
Lk 7:15 (AMP)

Joel
(Joel 2:13)

"God, who knows the heart, showed that he accepted them by giving the Holy Spirit to them, just as he did to us."
Ac 15:5-12 (NIV)
[Ac 10:36-46]

Joel 2:24 Threshing floor

2 Chronicles 22-25
(2Ch 23:3)

"...'Joseph, son of David,' the angel said, 'do not be afraid to take Mary as your wife. For the child within her was conceived by the Holy Spirit...'"
Mt 1:1, 18-25 (NLT)
[Is 7:14; Lk 1:32, 33]

2 Kings 11-14
(2Ki 13:20, 21)

"The tombs were opened, and many bodies of the saints who had fallen asleep were raised..."
Mt 27:50-54 (NASB)

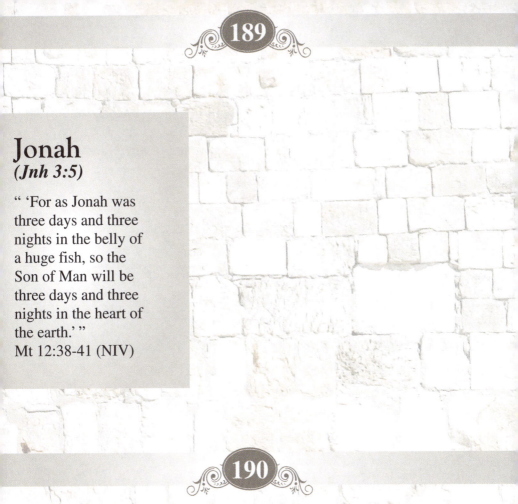

Jonah
(Jnh 3:5)

" 'For as Jonah was three days and three nights in the belly of a huge fish, so the Son of Man will be three days and three nights in the heart of the earth.' "
Mt 12:38-41 (NIV)

Amos 1-3
(Am 3:8)

"...the Lion that is from the tribe of Judah, the root of David, has overcome..."
Rev 5:4, 5 (NASB)

Amos 1:1 Sheep in the Tekoa and Herodium region

Amos 4-6
(Am 5:4)

"...and they followed Jesus. And Jesus turned ...and said to them, 'What do you seek?'..." "...Andrew, Simon Peter's brother...said to him, 'We have found the Messiah' (which translated means Christ)."
Jn 1:35-41 (NASB)

Amos 7-9
(Am 9:11, 12)

"...I will return and rebuild David's fallen tent...that the remnant of men may seek the Lord...'"
Ac 15:14-18   (NIV)

Amos 9:13 Plowed field

2 Chronicles 26-29
(2Ch 26:5)

"...I pray that in all respects you may prosper and be in good health, just as your soul prospers."
"...walking in truth."
3Jn 1:2, 3, 11 (NASB)

2Ch 28:15 Jericho, "the city of palm trees"

2 Kings 15-17
(2Ki 17:33)

"...what union can there be between God's temple and idols?..." 2Co 6:14-18 (NLT) [Eze 37:22-28; Is 43:6, 7; Jer 3:16-22]

2 Kings 18-20
(2Ki 19:19)

"...hallowed (kept holy) be Your name. Your kingdom come, Your will be done on earth as it is in heaven."
Mt 6:9, 10 (AMP)

2Ki 20:7 Fig tree near Bethlehem, one of the seven species in Deut 8:7, 8

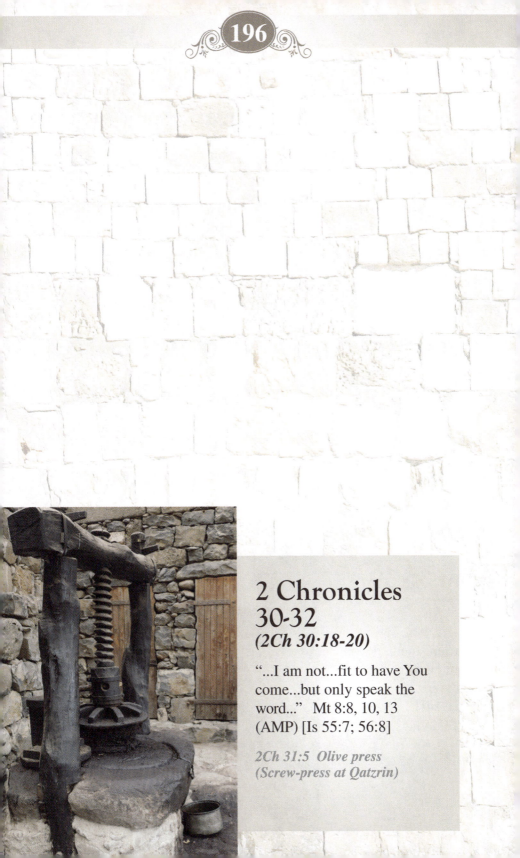

2 Chronicles 30-32
(2Ch 30:18-20)

"...I am not...fit to have You come...but only speak the word..." Mt 8:8, 10, 13 (AMP) [Is 55:7; 56:8]

2Ch 31:5 Olive press (Screw-press at Qatzrin)

Isaiah 36-39
(Is 37:32)

"Now there were Jews living in Jerusalem, devout men from every nation under heaven..."
Ac 2:5, 6, 14-18 (NASB)
[Joel 2:28, 29]

Is 38:21 Fig tree in Judah

2 Kings 21
(2Ki 21:7; Ex 34:13, 14)

"Do you think the Scriptures have no meaning? They say that God is passionate that the spirit he has placed within us should be faithful to him." James 4:5 (NLT)

Isa 59:21
Eze 11:19, 20
Eze 13:3
Eze 36:25-27

Hosea 2:17
Haggai 1:14
Zech 4:6
Zech 12:10

Hosea 1-4
(Hos 1:10)

"...not only from among Jews, but also from among Gentiles...they shall be called sons of the living God." Ro 9:24-26 (AMP) [1 Pe 2:9, 10]

Hosea 2:18
Bee-eaters in flight

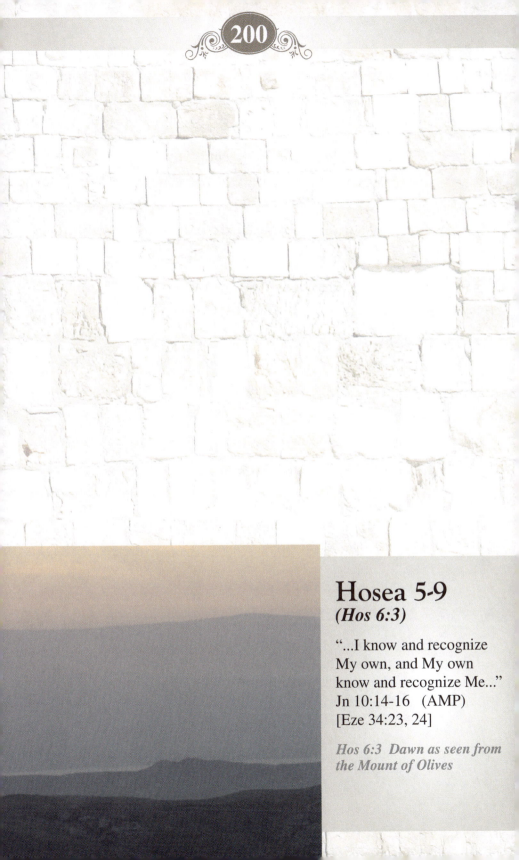

Hosea 5-9
(Hos 6:3)

"...I know and recognize My own, and My own know and recognize Me..." Jn 10:14-16 (AMP) [Eze 34:23, 24]

Hos 6:3 Dawn as seen from the Mount of Olives

Hosea 10-14
(Hos 11:1)

"...so was fulfilled what the Lord had said through the prophet: 'Out of Egypt I called my son.'"
Mt 2:13-15   (NIV)
[Jn 10:24, 25, 37, 38]

Hos 10:12   Woman reaping

Micah 1-4
(Mic 4:2)

"Simon Peter answered him, 'Lord, to whom shall we go? You have the words of eternal life.'"
Jn 6:67-69   (NIV)

Micah 2:12
Sheep gathered in a fold

Micah 5-7
(Mic 5:2)

"...and anxiously asked them where the Christ was to be born. They replied to him, In Bethlehem of Judea..." Mt 2:4-6 (AMP) [Ge 49:10; Ps 60:7; Lk 1:31, 32; Lk 2:11, 15, 21]

Mic 1:1 Shephelah of Judah; region of Micah's hometown, Moresheth (Moresheth-gath)

Isaiah 1-3
(Is 1:18)

" '...There is the Lamb of God, who takes away the sin of the world!' " Jn 1:29 (AMP)
[Ro 6:23; 1Jn 1:7; 1Jn 2:1, 2; 3:5]

Is 1:3 Donkey walking ahead of master because it knows the way

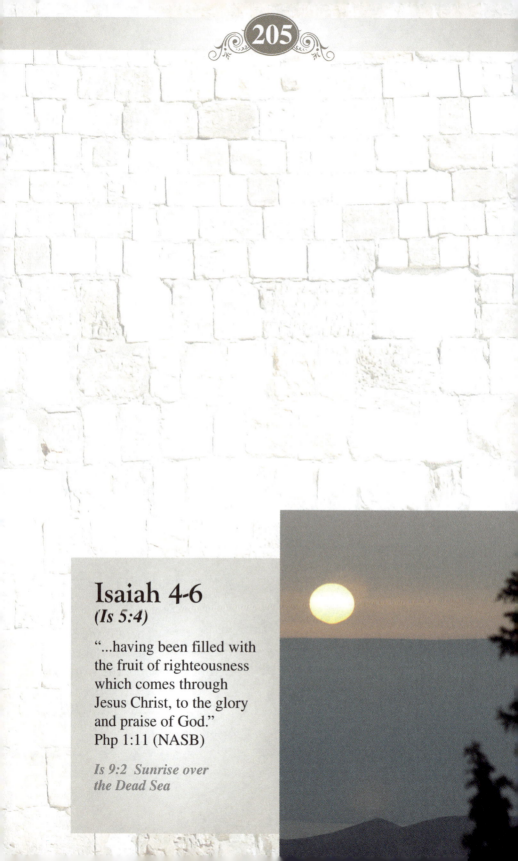

Isaiah 4-6
(Is 5:4)

"...having been filled with the fruit of righteousness which comes through Jesus Christ, to the glory and praise of God."
Php 1:11 (NASB)

Is 9:2 Sunrise over the Dead Sea

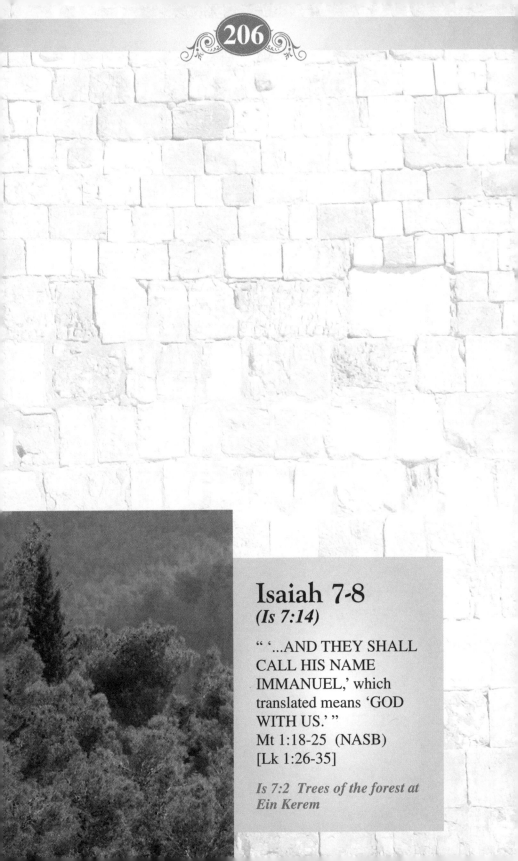

Isaiah 7-8
(Is 7:14)

" '...AND THEY SHALL CALL HIS NAME IMMANUEL,' which translated means 'GOD WITH US.' "
Mt 1:18-25 (NASB)
[Lk 1:26-35]

Is 7:2 Trees of the forest at Ein Kerem

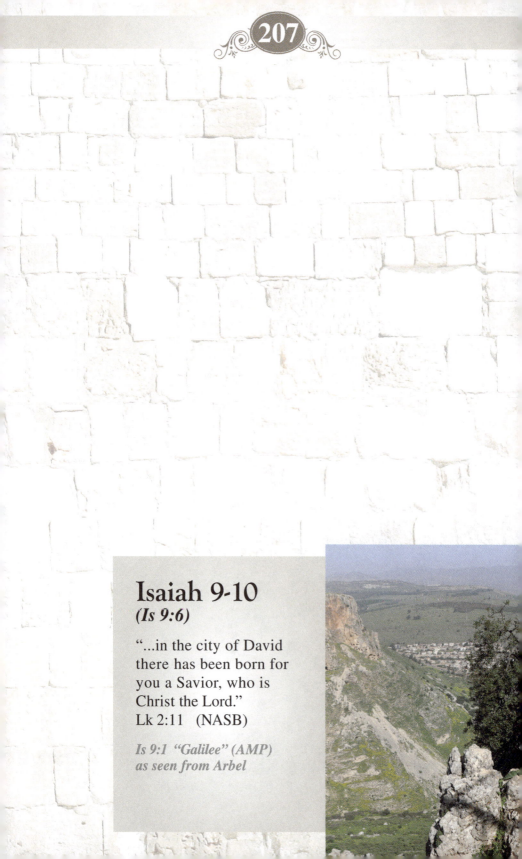

Isaiah 9-10
(Is 9:6)

"...in the city of David there has been born for you a Savior, who is Christ the Lord."
Lk 2:11   (NASB)

Is 9:1 "Galilee" (AMP) as seen from Arbel

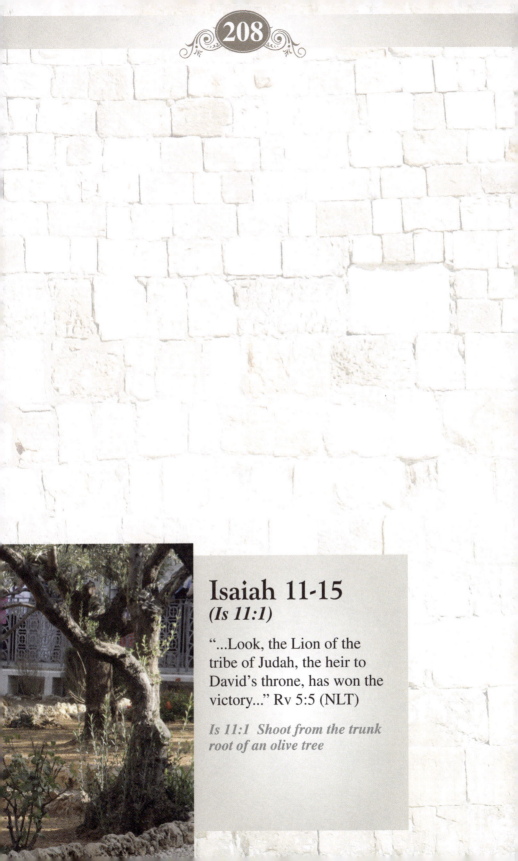

Isaiah 11-15
(Is 11:1)

"...Look, the Lion of the tribe of Judah, the heir to David's throne, has won the victory..." Rv 5:5 (NLT)

Is 11:1 Shoot from the trunk root of an olive tree

Isaiah 16-18
(Is 16:5)

"...to the Son, He says to Him, Your throne, O God, is forever and ever...and the scepter of Your kingdom is a scepter of absolute righteousness..."
Heb 1:8 (AMP)
[Ps 45:6, 7]

Isaiah 19-22
(Is 22:9b-11a)

Jesus said: "...'Go wash in the Pool of Siloam' – which means Sent. So he went and washed and came back seeing."
Jn 9:7 (AMP)

Isaiah 23-26
(Is 25:8; Hosea 13:14)

"...then shall be fulfilled the Scripture that says, 'Death is swallowed up (utterly vanquished forever) in and unto victory.'"
1Co 15:54-57 (AMP)
[Rv 21:3, 4]

Is 26:19 Dew clouds in the Jordan Valley

Isaiah 27-29
(Is 28:16; Ps 118:22)

"...the living Stone - rejected by men but chosen by God and precious to him..."
" '...See, I lay a stone in Zion, a...precious cornerstone...' "
1Pe 2:4-7a (NIV)

Is 27:3 Watchtower

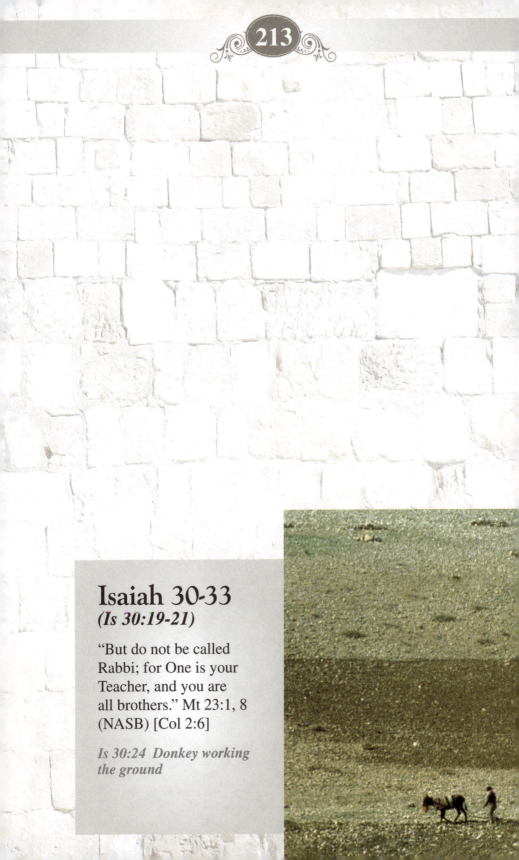

Isaiah 30-33
(Is 30:19-21)

"But do not be called Rabbi; for One is your Teacher, and you are all brothers." Mt 23:1, 8 (NASB) [Col 2:6]

Is 30:24 Donkey working the ground

Isaiah 34-35
(Is 35:5, 6)

"...'Go back to John and tell him what you have heard and seen – the blind see, the lame walk, the lepers are cured, the deaf hear...' " Mt 11:2-6 (NLT) [Ac 3:1-6]

Is 35:6 Stream in the desert at Wadi Arugot

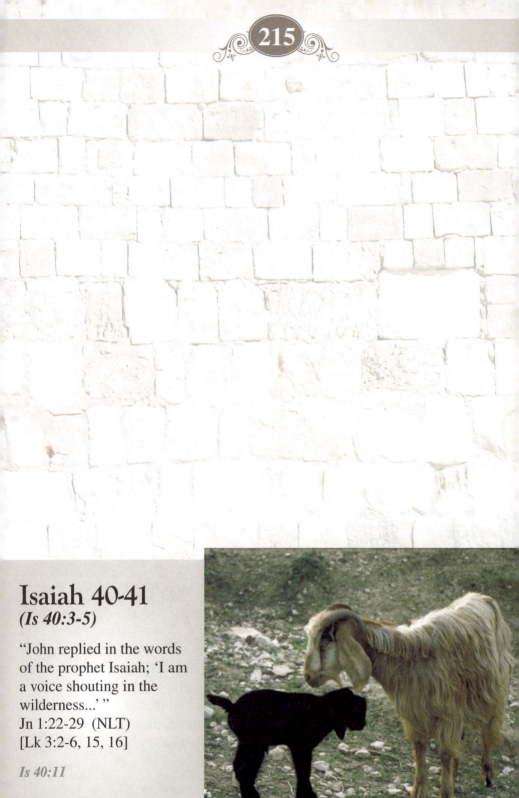

Isaiah 40-41
(Is 40:3-5)

"John replied in the words of the prophet Isaiah; 'I am a voice shouting in the wilderness...' "
Jn 1:22-29 (NLT)
[Lk 3:2-6, 15, 16]

Is 40:11

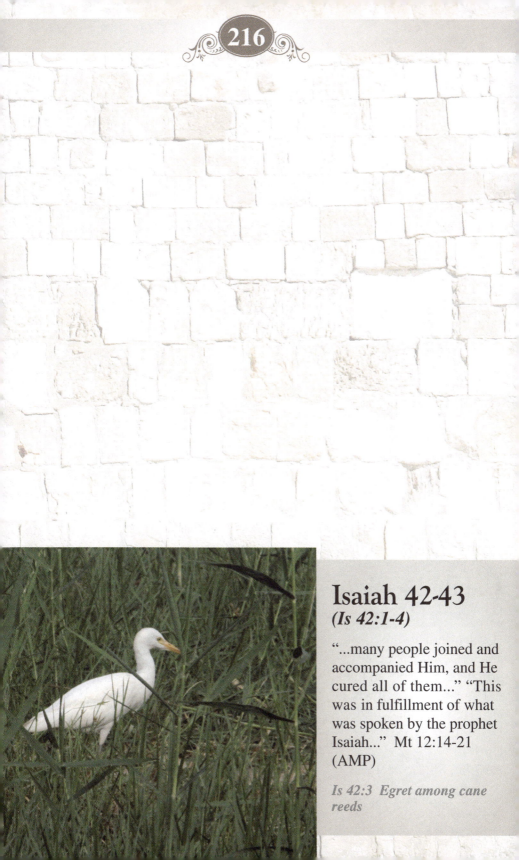

Isaiah 42-43
(Is 42:1-4)

"...many people joined and accompanied Him, and He cured all of them..." "This was in fulfillment of what was spoken by the prophet Isaiah..." Mt 12:14-21 (AMP)

Is 42:3 Egret among cane reeds

Isaiah 44-48
(Is 48:12, 13)

"God, after He spoke long ago to the fathers in the prophets...has spoken to us in His Son...through whom also He made the world." Heb 1:1, 2 (NASB) [Jn 1:15; *Stephen:* Ac 7:55, 56; Col 2:9]

Is 44:23 Mountain forest of Ein Kerem

Isaiah 49-51
(Is 51:6;
Ps 102:25-27)

"Sky and earth will pass away, but My words will not pass away."
Mt 24:1, 2, 35 (AMP)
[Heb 1:2, 3, 10-12]

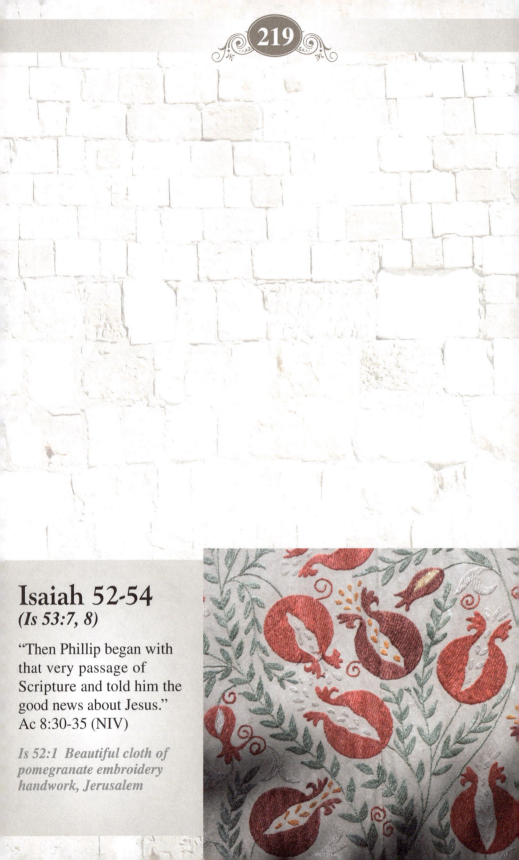

Isaiah 52-54
(Is 53:7, 8)

"Then Phillip began with that very passage of Scripture and told him the good news about Jesus."
Ac 8:30-35 (NIV)

Is 52:1 Beautiful cloth of pomegranate embroidery handwork, Jerusalem

Isaiah 55-58
(Is 55:1)

"And let the one who is thirsty come; let the one who wishes take the water of life without cost."
Rev 22:16, 17 (NASB)

Is 58:11 A watered garden at Hamat Gadar

Isaiah 59-60
(Is 59:16; Col 2:9)

"...if anyone should sin, we have an Advocate (One Who will intercede for us) with the Father – [it is] Jesus Christ [the all] righteous..."
1Jn 1:1-3; 2:1, 2 (AMP)
[Ro 8:33, 34]

Is 60:8 Dove in flight

Isaiah 61-64
(Is 61:1)

Jesus said: "The Spirit of the Lord [is] upon Me, because he has anointed Me...to preach the good news...to announce release to the captives..."
Lk 4:14-21 (AMP)

Is 61:3 Oak trees at Caesarea Philippi

Isaiah 65-66
(Is 65:17)

"But we are looking forward to the new heavens and the new earth he has promised..."
2Pe 1:1, 2; 3:13 (NLT)

Nahum
(Na 1:7)

Jesus speaks: " 'I am the good shepherd; I know my own sheep and they know me...' "
Jn 10:7, 10, 14 (NLT)

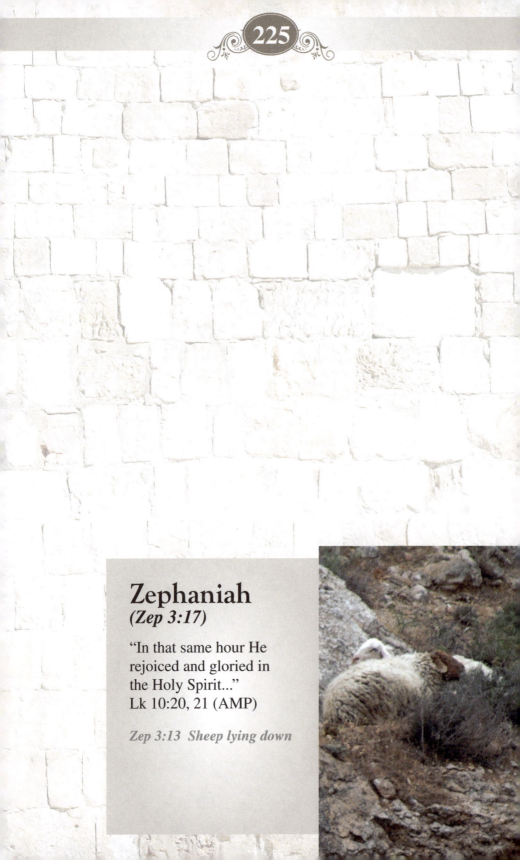

Zephaniah
(Zep 3:17)

"In that same hour He rejoiced and gloried in the Holy Spirit..."
Lk 10:20, 21 (AMP)

Zep 3:13 Sheep lying down

Habakkuk
(Hab 2:4)

"Clearly no one is justified before God by the law, because, 'The righteous will live by faith.'"
Gal 3:5-14 (NIV)

Hab 3:17
Horse among olive trees

Obadiah
(Ob vs 21b)

"...and the kingdom and the kingship shall be the Lord's."
"...He will reign over the house of Jacob throughout the ages; and of His reign there will be no end."
Lk 1:31-35 (AMP)
[Is 9:6, 7; Dan 2:44]

2 Kings 22-25
(2Ki 22:8)

"And take...the sword of the Spirit, which is the Word of God."
Eph 6:10-17 (NASB)

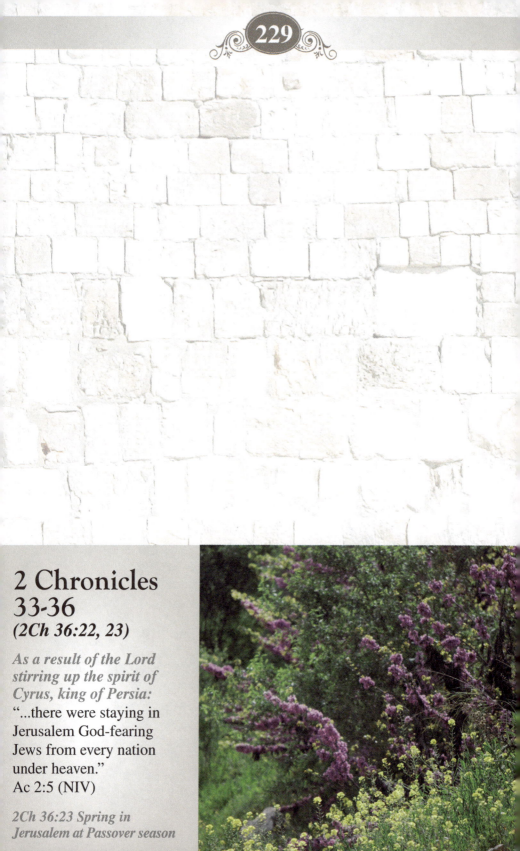

2 Chronicles 33-36
(2Ch 36:22, 23)

As a result of the Lord stirring up the spirit of Cyrus, king of Persia: "...there were staying in Jerusalem God-fearing Jews from every nation under heaven." Ac 2:5 (NIV)

2Ch 36:23 Spring in Jerusalem at Passover season

Jeremiah 1-3
(Jer 2:13)

Jesus said: " '...the water that I will give him shall become a spring of water welling up...within him...unto...eternal life.' "
Jn 4:5-10, 13, 14 (AMP)
[Jn 7:2, 37, 38]

Jer 1:11 Almond trees blooming on the Mount of Olives

Jeremiah 4-5
(Jer 4:4a)

"...true circumcision is not merely obeying the letter of the law; rather, it is a change of heart produced by the Spirit." "...a changed heart seeks praise from God, not from people."
Ro 2:28-29 (NLT)

Jer 4:3 Plowed ground in Judah

Jeremiah 6-8
(Jer 6:16)

"...Let me teach you, because I am humble and gentle at heart, and you will find rest for your souls.'"
Mt 11:28-29   (NLT)

Jer 8:7 "...the swallow..." (NLT) A singing swallow has returned in spring to the Sea of Galilee

Jeremiah 9-12
(Jer 9:23, 24)

"...Christ Jesus...is our righteousness, holiness and redemption. Therefore ...'Let him who boasts boast in the Lord.'"
1Co 1:29-31 (NIV)
[Ps 73:25, 26; Jn 6:62-64, 67-69]

Jeremiah 13-16
(Jer 14:22)

"Such hope never disappoints or deludes or shames us, for God's love has been poured out in our hearts through the Holy Spirit Who has been given to us." Ro 5:1-5 (AMP)

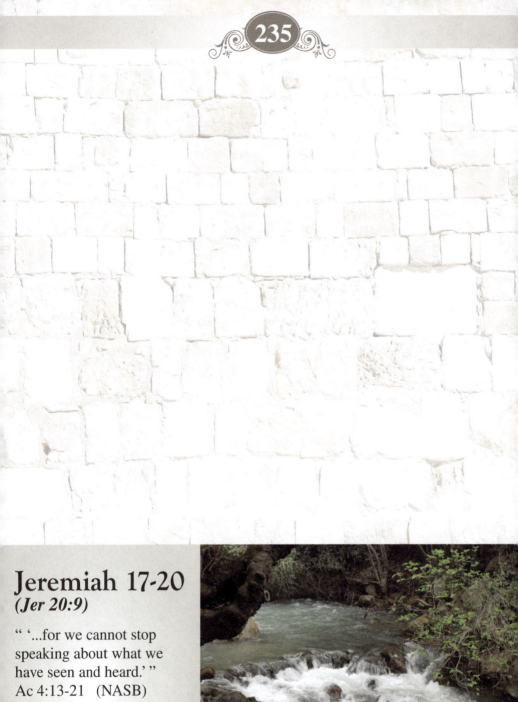

Jeremiah 17-20
(Jer 20:9)

" '...for we cannot stop speaking about what we have seen and heard.' "
Ac 4:13-21   (NASB)

Jer 17:13
"Fountain of living water..."
Caesarea Philippi region

Jeremiah 21-24
(Jer 23:6)

"But now apart from the Law the righteousness of God has been manifested, being witnessed by the Law and the Prophets, even the righteousness of God through faith..." Ro 3:21, 22 (NASB)

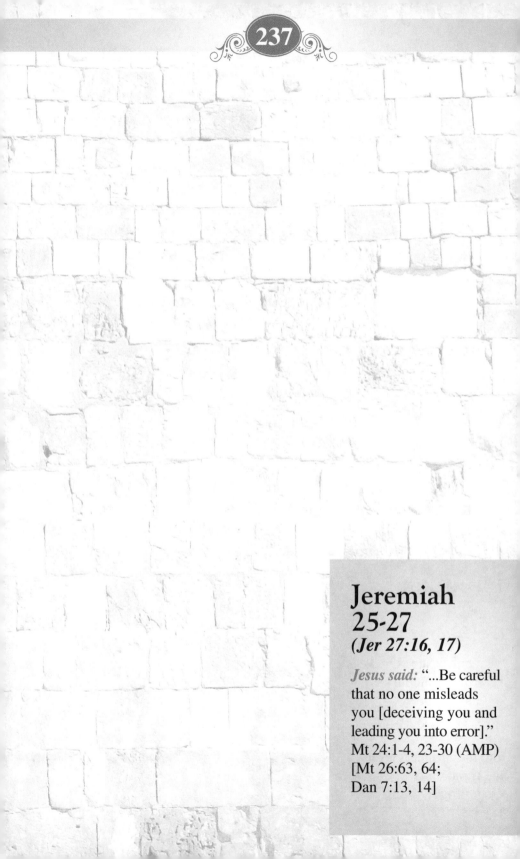

Jeremiah 25-27
(Jer 27:16, 17)

Jesus said: "...Be careful that no one misleads you [deceiving you and leading you into error]."
Mt 24:1-4, 23-30 (AMP)
[Mt 26:63, 64; Dan 7:13, 14]

Jeremiah 28-30
(Jer 30:9)

"...he shouted all the more, 'Son of David, have mercy on me!' "
Lk 18:35-42 (NIV)
[Jer 33:14, 15]

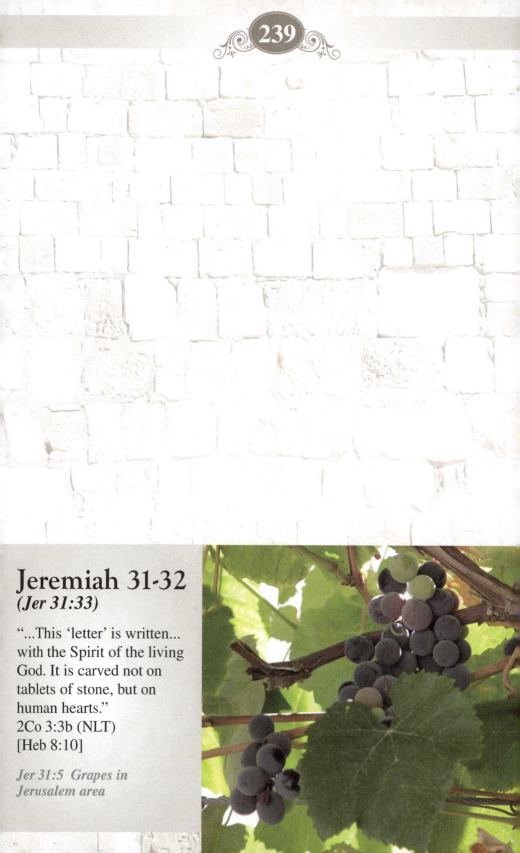

Jeremiah 31-32
(Jer 31:33)

"...This 'letter' is written... with the Spirit of the living God. It is carved not on tablets of stone, but on human hearts."
2Co 3:3b (NLT)
[Heb 8:10]

Jer 31:5 Grapes in Jerusalem area

Jeremiah 33-36
(Jer 33:15)

From Egypt to Nazareth: "...spoken through the prophets..." "He shall be called a Nazarene [Branch, Separated One]." Mt 2:23 (AMP) [Is 11:1]

Jer 33:13 Sheep in Judah

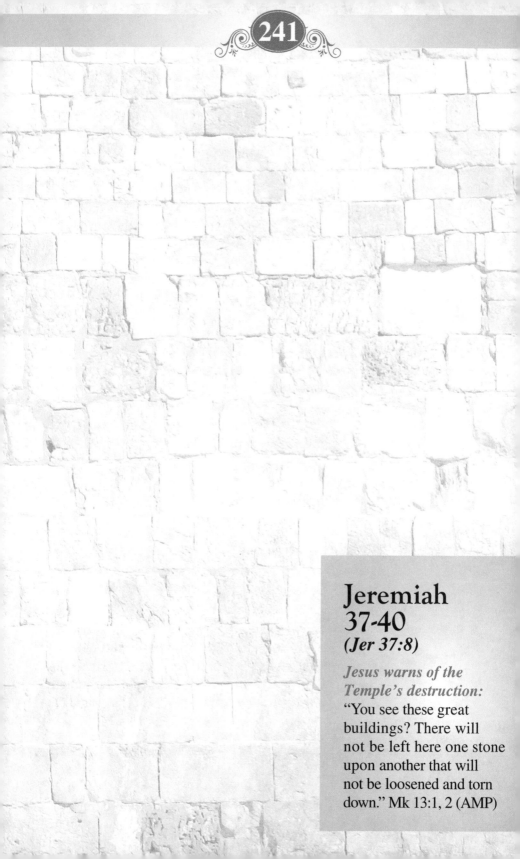

Jeremiah 37-40
(Jer 37:8)

Jesus warns of the Temple's destruction: "You see these great buildings? There will not be left here one stone upon another that will not be loosened and torn down." Mk 13:1, 2 (AMP)

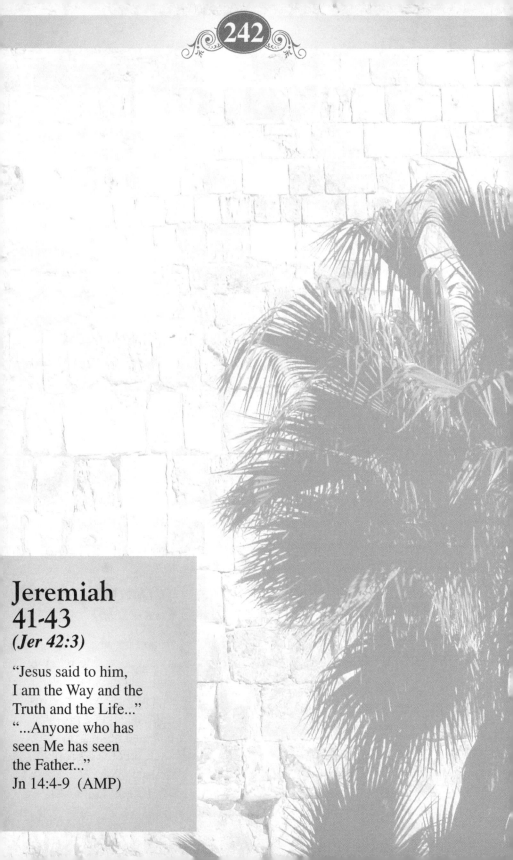

Jeremiah 41-43
(Jer 42:3)

"Jesus said to him, I am the Way and the Truth and the Life..."
"...Anyone who has seen Me has seen the Father..."
Jn 14:4-9 (AMP)

Jeremiah 44-48
(Jer 44:16)

"...and he who receives... and accepts Me receives and...accepts Him Who sent Me. He who receives and...accepts a prophet because he is a prophet shall receive a prophet's reward..."
Mt 10:40, 41a (AMP)

Jeremiah 49
(Jer 49:1)

The Decapolis includes the tribal territory of Gad, son of Jacob:
"Large crowds from Galilee, the Decapolis, Jerusalem, Judea and the region across the Jordan followed him."
Mt 4:23-25 (NIV)

Jeremiah 50
(Jer 50:4, 5)

"Now the God of peace, who brought up from the dead the great Shepherd of the sheep through the blood of the eternal covenant...equip you in every good thing to do His will..." Heb 13:20, 21 (NASB) [Jer 31:31-33; 2Co 3:5, 6]

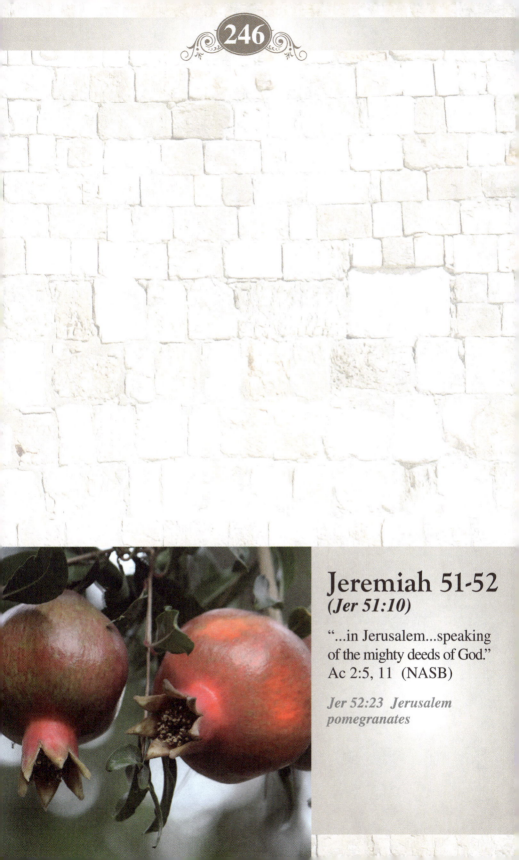

Jeremiah 51-52
(Jer 51:10)

"...in Jerusalem...speaking of the mighty deeds of God." Ac 2:5, 11 (NASB)

Jer 52:23 Jerusalem pomegranates

Lamentations
(La 1:4; Jer 22:1-5)

"O Jerusalem, Jerusalem...!" "How often would I have gathered your children together as a mother fowl gathers her brood under her wings, and you refused!"
Mt 23:37-38 (AMP)

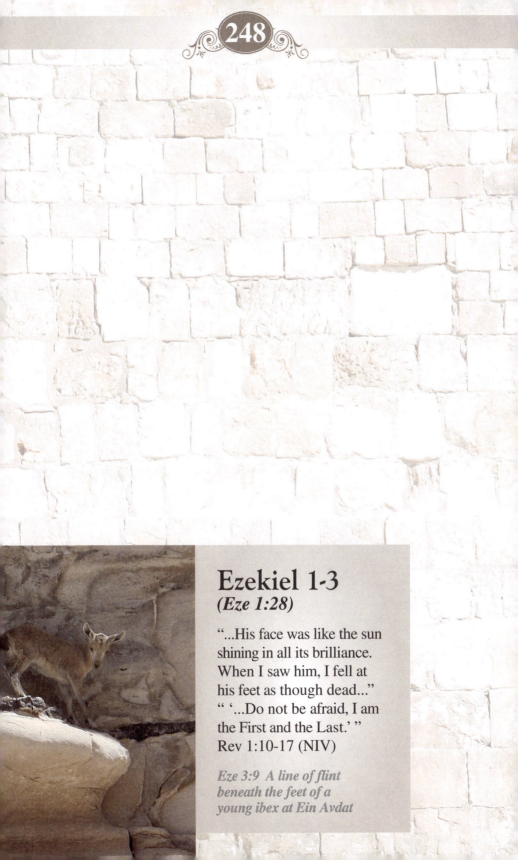

Ezekiel 1-3
(Eze 1:28)

"...His face was like the sun shining in all its brilliance. When I saw him, I fell at his feet as though dead..."
" '...Do not be afraid, I am the First and the Last.' "
Rev 1:10-17 (NIV)

Eze 3:9 A line of flint beneath the feet of a young ibex at Ein Avdat

Ezekiel 4-7
(Eze 7:19)

" '...Silver or gold I do not have, but what I have I give you...' "
Ac 3:1-16 (NIV)

Ezekiel 8-10
(Eze 8:2)

"...His feet glowed like burnished (bright) bronze..." "...and His face was like the sun shining in full power at midday."
Rv 1:9, 10, 15, 16 (AMP)

Ezekiel 11-15
(Eze 11:19, 20)

"...not written with ink but with [the] Spirit of the living God, not on tablets of stone but on tablets of human hearts."
2Co 3:2, 3 (AMP)

Eze 11:17 Shepherdess at harvest while her sheep are gathered and resting nearby

Ezekiel 16-17
(Eze 16:6)

" '...I came that they might have life, and have it abundantly.' "
Jn 10:10b (NASB)

Eze 16:13
Embroidered cloth

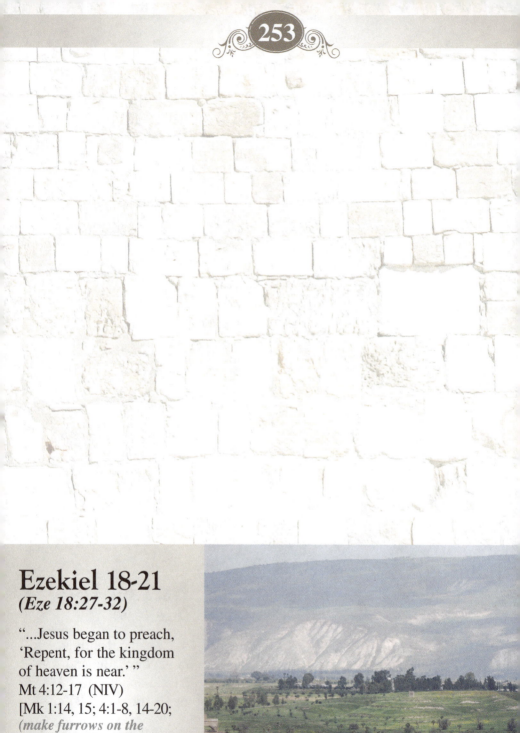

Ezekiel 18-21
(Eze 18:27-32)

"...Jesus began to preach, 'Repent, for the kingdom of heaven is near.'"
Mt 4:12-17 (NIV)
[Mk 1:14, 15; 4:1-8, 14-20; *(make furrows on the land of your hearts)*
"Break up your unplowed ground..." Jer 4:3]

Eze 20:42 Jordan River Valley; part of "the land"

Ezekiel 22-24
(Eze 22:15)

"...praising God..."
"...the Lord was adding to their number day by day..." Ac 2:5, 43-47 (NASB)

Ezekiel 25-28
(Eze 28:25)

" 'Here we are – Parthians, Medes, Elamites, people from Mesopotamia, Judea, Cappadocia, Pontus, the province of Asia, Phrygia, Pamphylia, Egypt...areas of Libya around Cyrene...Rome (both Jews and converts to Judaism), Cretans, and Arabs...' " Ac 2:5-11 (NLT)

Eze 27:17 Honeybee

Ezekiel 29-31
(Eze 29:21)

"...He has raised up a horn of salvation for us in the house of his servant David..."
Lk 1:57, 67-69 (NIV)

Ezekiel 32-33
(Eze 33:30)

"...Philip replied, Come and see!"
Jn 1:45, 46 (AMP)

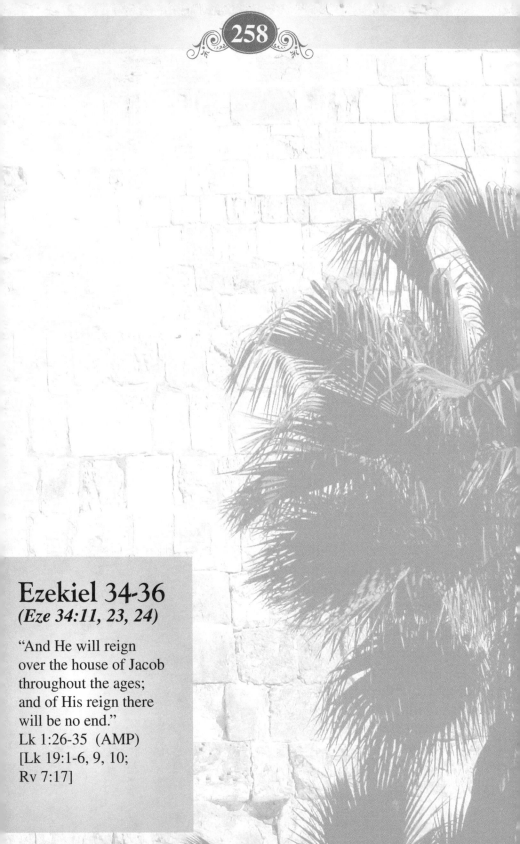

Ezekiel 34-36
(Eze 34:11, 23, 24)

"And He will reign over the house of Jacob throughout the ages; and of His reign there will be no end."
Lk 1:26-35 (AMP)
[Lk 19:1-6, 9, 10; Rv 7:17]

Ezekiel 37-39
(Eze 37:26)

"...May the God of peace – who brought up from the dead our Lord Jesus, the great Shepherd of the sheep, and ratified an eternal covenant with his blood...equip you..." Heb 13:20, 21 (NLT)

Eze 37:24 "...and they will have one shepherd."

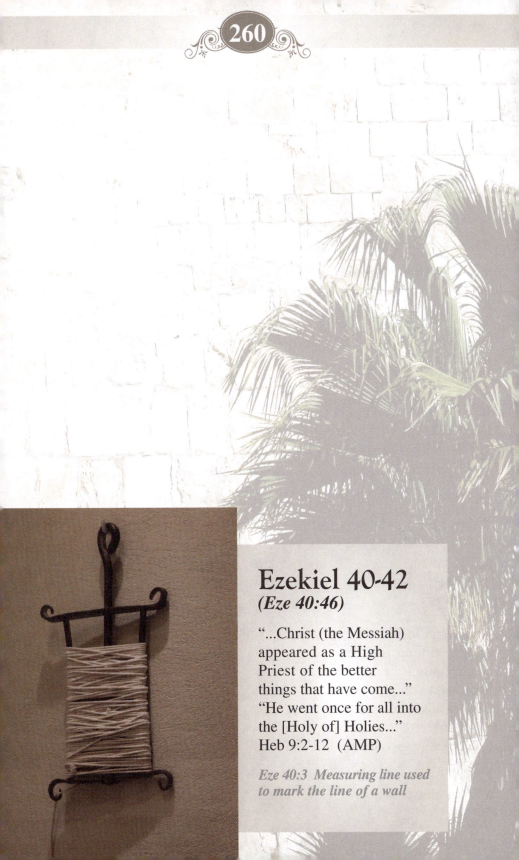

Ezekiel 40-42
(Eze 40:46)

"...Christ (the Messiah) appeared as a High Priest of the better things that have come..." "He went once for all into the [Holy of] Holies..." Heb 9:2-12 (AMP)

Eze 40:3 Measuring line used to mark the line of a wall

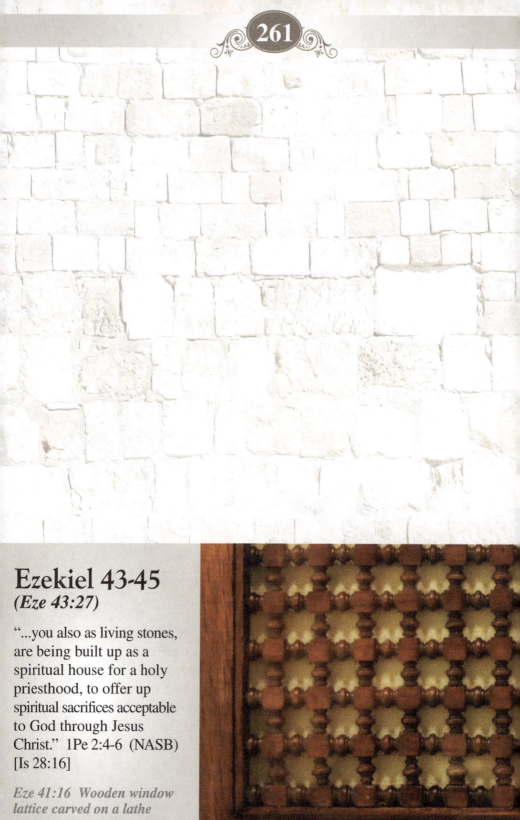

Ezekiel 43-45
(Eze 43:27)

"...you also as living stones, are being built up as a spiritual house for a holy priesthood, to offer up spiritual sacrifices acceptable to God through Jesus Christ." 1Pe 2:4-6 (NASB) [Is 28:16]

Eze 41:16 Wooden window lattice carved on a lathe

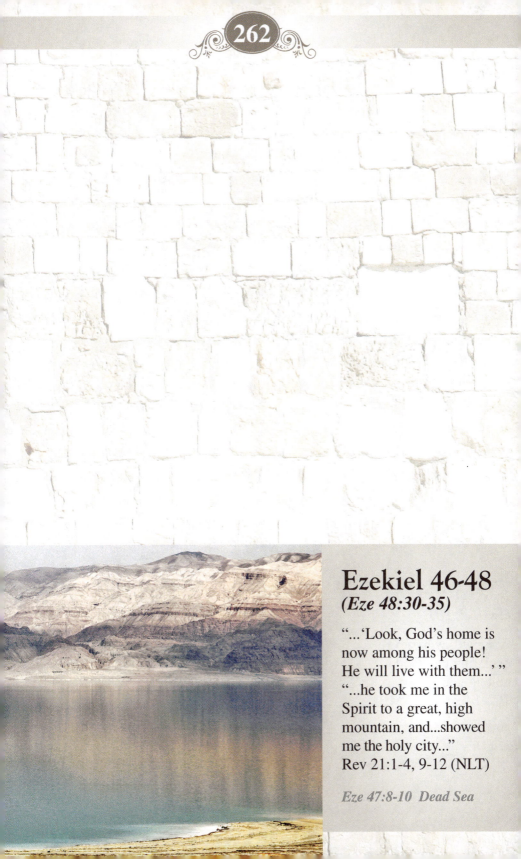

Ezekiel 46-48
(Eze 48:30-35)

"...'Look, God's home is now among his people! He will live with them...'"
"...he took me in the Spirit to a great, high mountain, and...showed me the holy city..."
Rev 21:1-4, 9-12 (NLT)

Eze 47:8-10 Dead Sea

Daniel 1-3
(Dan 2:10)

"...he will worship God, declaring that God is among you in very truth."
1Co 14:24, 25 (AMP)

Dan 2:35 Threshing floor near Bethlehem

Daniel 4-6
(Dan 4:2, 3)

" '...a Man...attested to you by God by the mighty works and...wonders and signs...' "
Ac 2:22-24 (AMP)
[Mt 12:22-28]

Dan 5:21 Wild Ass, native of the region of ancient Babylon; a type of Onager at Hai Bar Nature Reserve

Daniel 7-9
(Dan 7:13, 14)

"He is coming with the clouds, and every eye will see Him..."
Rv 1:7 (AMP)

Daniel 10-12
(Dan 10:1)

Daniel is among these prophets: "Indeed, all the prophets from Samuel on, as many as have spoken, have foretold these days." Ac 3:1, 2, 9-16, 24-26 (NIV) [Ge 22:18; Gal 3:16; Rv 11:15]

Ezra 1-5
(Ezra 1:3)

"...He had spoken of the temple which was His body." "When...He had risen from the dead, His disciples remembered that He said this..." Jn 2:18-22 (AMP) [Mk 14:55-62; Dan 7:13, 14; Rv 1:4-7]

Ezra 2:67 Donkey and colt

Haggai
(Hag 1:13)

"...be encouraged and consoled and comforted; be of the same [agreeable] mind one with another; live in peace, and [then] the God of love...and the Author and Promoter of peace will be with you."
2Co 13:11 (AMP)

Zechariah 1-5
(Zec 3:8, 9; 4:10)

"...I saw a lamb standing, as though it had been slain, with seven horns and with seven eyes, which are the seven Spirits of God [the sevenfold Holy Spirit]..." Rev 5:5, 6 (AMP)

Zec 4:3 Olive trees

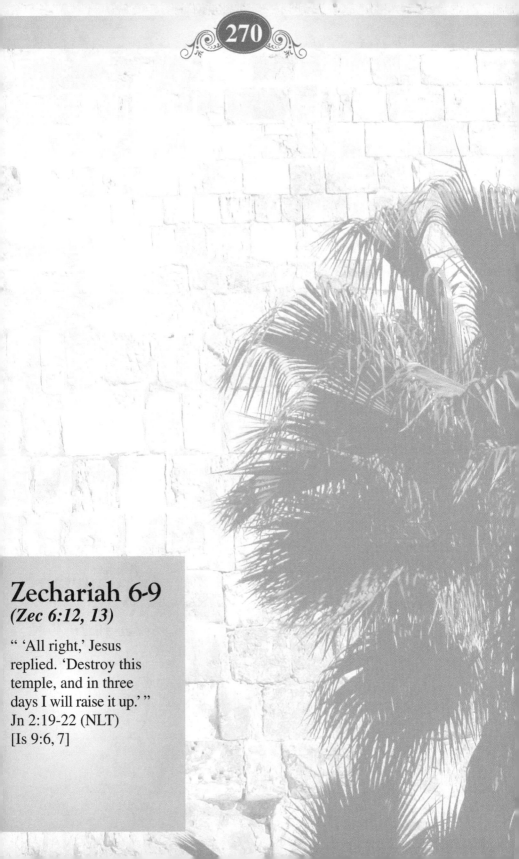

Zechariah 6-9
(Zec 6:12, 13)

" 'All right,' Jesus replied. 'Destroy this temple, and in three days I will raise it up.' "
Jn 2:19-22 (NLT)
[Is 9:6, 7]

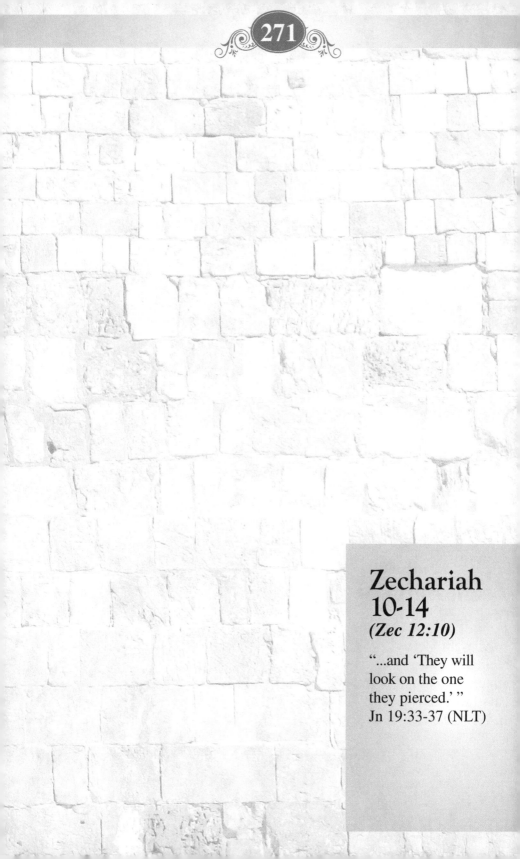

Zechariah 10-14
(Zec 12:10)

"...and 'They will look on the one they pierced.'"
Jn 19:33-37 (NLT)

Ezra 6-10
(Ezra 6:19, 20)

"...John saw Jesus coming to him and said, Look! There is the Lamb of God, Who takes away the sin of the world!"
Jn 1:24-34 (AMP)
[Mal 3:1, 4:5; Mt 11:1, 9, 10, 14; Mt 17:1, 10-13]

Ezra 7:6 Stylus made of cane reed at Qatzrin

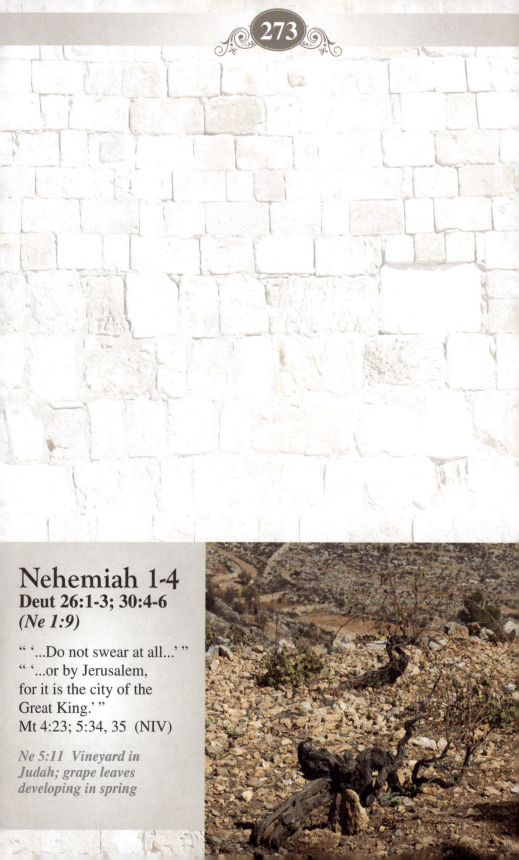

Nehemiah 1-4
Deut 26:1-3; 30:4-6
(Ne 1:9)

" '...Do not swear at all...' "
" '...or by Jerusalem, for it is the city of the Great King.' "
Mt 4:23; 5:34, 35 (NIV)

Ne 5:11 Vineyard in Judah; grape leaves developing in spring

Nehemiah 5-8
(Ne 8:13, 14)

"Now on the final and most important day of the Feast, Jesus stood, and He cried in a loud voice, If any man is thirsty, let him come to Me and drink!" Jn 7:2, 37, 38 (AMP) [Jer 2:13; Rv 22:16, 17]

Ne 5:11 Olive grove in Jerusalem

Nehemiah 9-10
(Ne 9:15a)

"Jesus replied, I am the Bread of Life. He who comes to Me will never be hungry..."
Jn 6:30-35, 47-51 (AMP)

Ne 10:37 Stone Pine, Jerusalem; a pine nut producing tree

Nehemiah 11-13
(Ne 12:46)

"...but be filled with the spirit, speaking to one another in psalms and hymns and spiritual songs...giving thanks..."
Eph 5:6-20 (NASB)
[Is 59:20, 21; 60:1, 2; Rv 21:10, 22, 23]

Ne 11:31 Michmash area

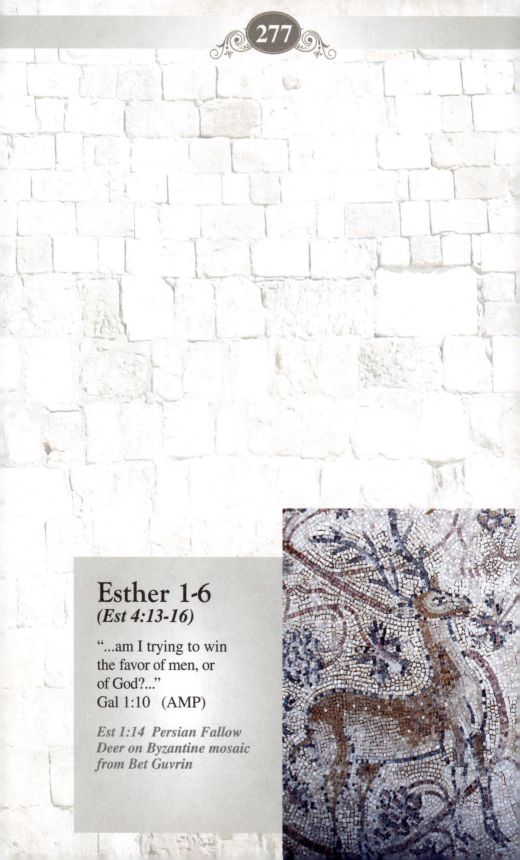

Esther 1-6
(Est 4:13-16)

"...am I trying to win the favor of men, or of God?..."
Gal 1:10 (AMP)

Est 1:14 Persian Fallow Deer on Byzantine mosaic from Bet Guvrin

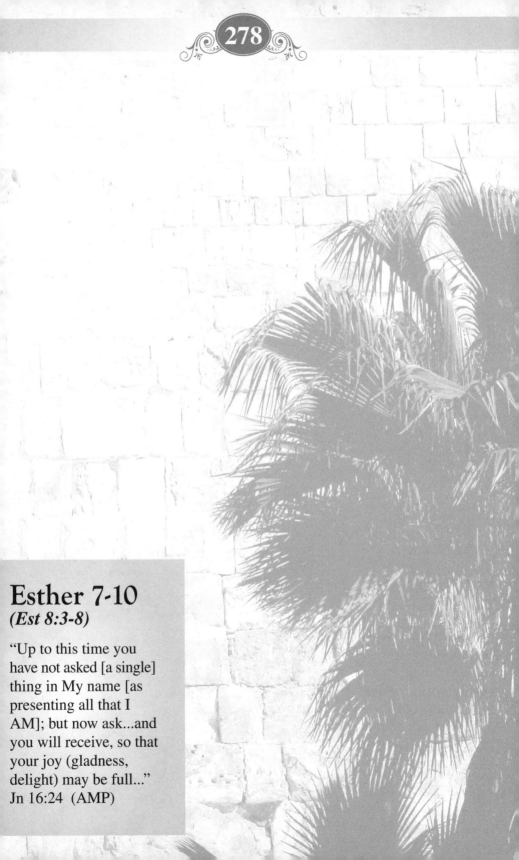

Esther 7-10
(Est 8:3-8)

"Up to this time you have not asked [a single] thing in My name [as presenting all that I AM]; but now ask...and you will receive, so that your joy (gladness, delight) may be full..."
Jn 16:24 (AMP)

Malachi
(Mal 3:1)

"John is the man to whom the Scriptures refer when they say, 'Look, I am sending my messenger ahead of you...' "
Mt 11:7, 9, 10, 14 (NLT)
[Lk 1:13-17]

Mal 1:11 "...from the rising of the sun to its setting..." (AMP) Sky over Jerusalem

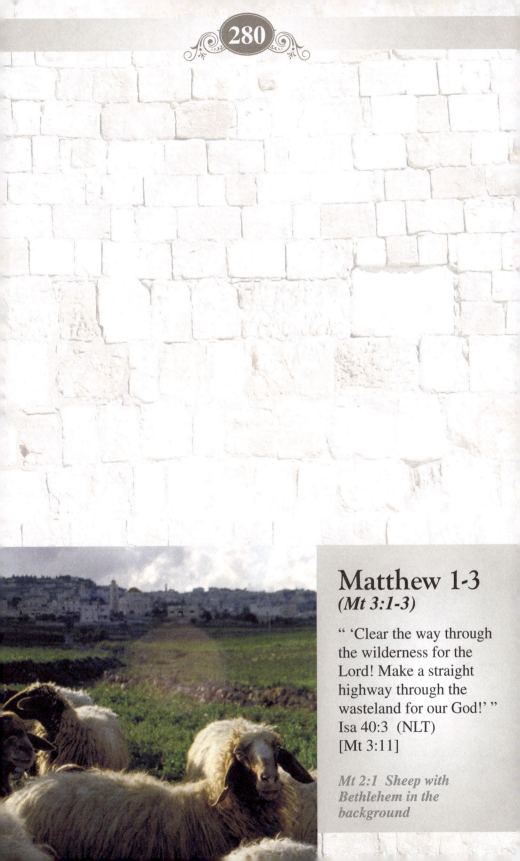

Matthew 1-3
(Mt 3:1-3)

" 'Clear the way through the wilderness for the Lord! Make a straight highway through the wasteland for our God!' "
Isa 40:3 (NLT)
[Mt 3:11]

Mt 2:1 Sheep with Bethlehem in the background

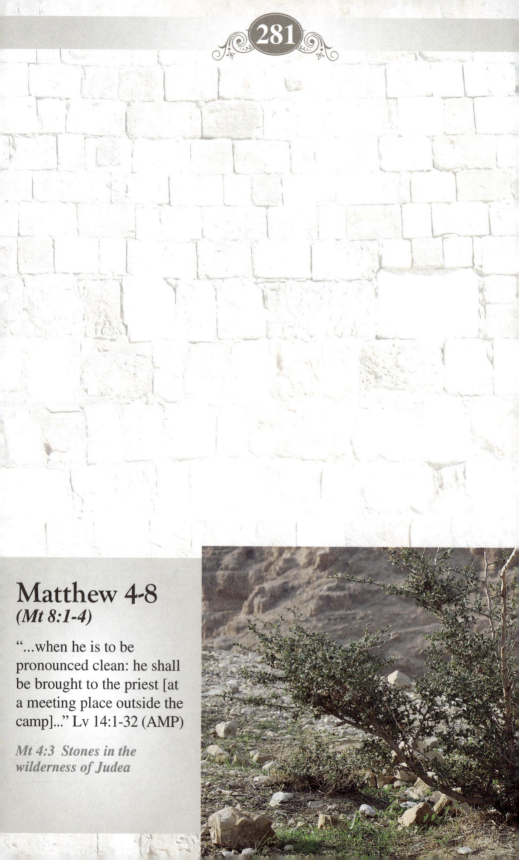

Matthew 4-8
(Mt 8:1-4)

"...when he is to be pronounced clean: he shall be brought to the priest [at a meeting place outside the camp]..." Lv 14:1-32 (AMP)

Mt 4:3 Stones in the wilderness of Judea

Matthew 9-11
(Mt 11:2-15)

" '...I will send my messenger, who will prepare the way before me.' " " '...suddenly the Lord you are seeking will come...' " Mal 3:1 (NIV)

Mt 9:1 Capernaum area at the Sea of Galilee

Matthew 12-13
(Mt 12:40)

"Now the Lord prepared and appointed a great fish to swallow up Jonah. And Jonah was in the belly of the fish three days and three nights."
Jnh 1:17 (AMP)

Mt 12:1 Heads of grain (NASB)

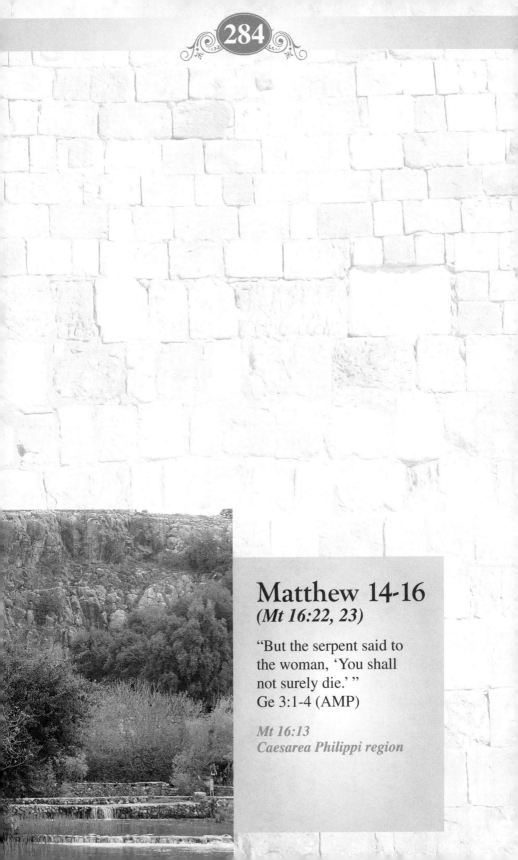

Matthew 14-16
(Mt 16:22, 23)

"But the serpent said to the woman, 'You shall not surely die.' "
Ge 3:1-4 (AMP)

*Mt 16:13
Caesarea Philippi region*

285

Matthew 17-20
(Mt 17:5)

"Behold, My Servant, whom I uphold; My chosen one in whom My soul delights."
Is 42:1 (NASB)

Mt 17:20 Mustard among King Solomon's Crown cyclamen

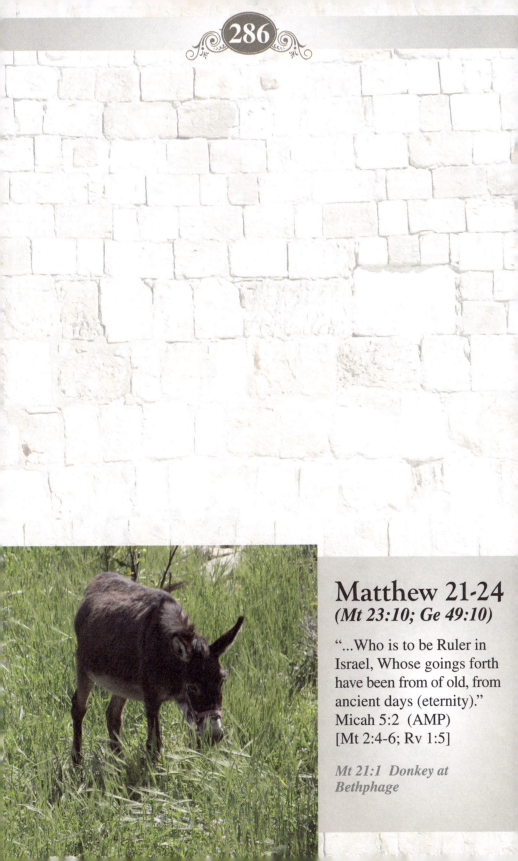

Matthew 21-24
(Mt 23:10; Ge 49:10)

"...Who is to be Ruler in Israel, Whose goings forth have been from of old, from ancient days (eternity)." Micah 5:2 (AMP)
[Mt 2:4-6; Rv 1:5]

Mt 21:1 Donkey at Bethphage

Matthew 25-28
(Mt 26:64)

"I saw someone like a Son of Man coming with the clouds of heaven. He approached the Ancient One..." Da 7:13, 14 (NLT)

Mt 25:35 A warm welcome

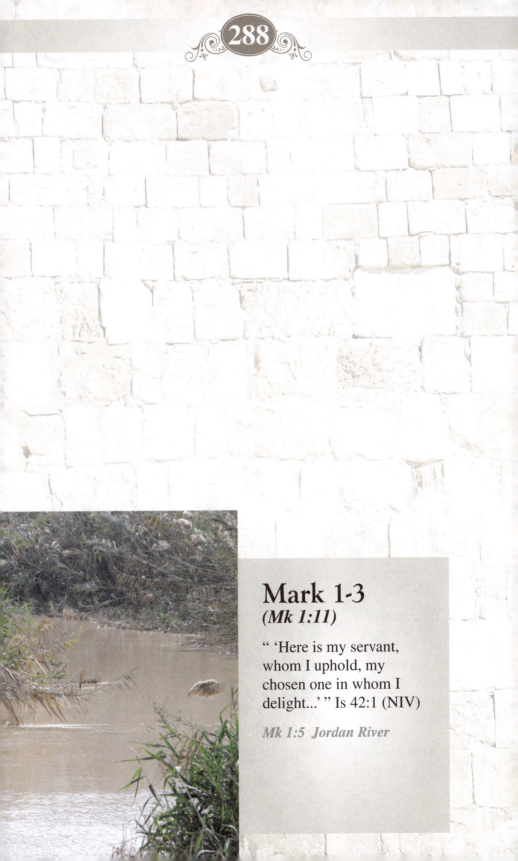

Mark 1-3
(Mk 1:11)

" 'Here is my servant, whom I uphold, my chosen one in whom I delight...' " Is 42:1 (NIV)

Mk 1:5 Jordan River

Mark 4-5
(Mk 4:7, 8; Jer 4:3)

" '...the LORD has sought out a man after his own heart...' "
1Sa 13:5-14 (NIV)
[Ps 119:10-16]

Mark 4:20 Field prepared for sowing

Mark 6-9
(Mk 6:39)

"He makes me lie down in [fresh, tender] green pastures..."
Ps 23:1, 2 (AMP)
[1Pe 2:24, 25; Heb 13:20, 21]

Mk 6:39 Green grass near the Sea of Galilee

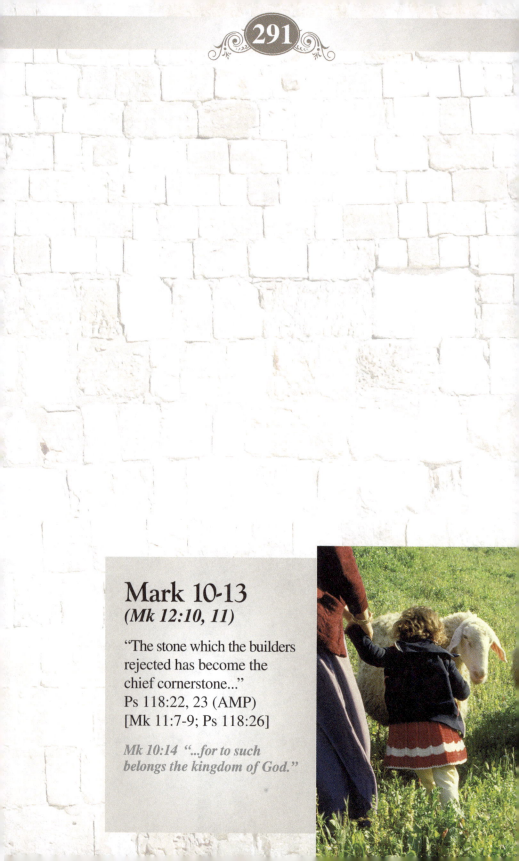

Mark 10-13
(Mk 12:10, 11)

"The stone which the builders rejected has become the chief cornerstone..."
Ps 118:22, 23 (AMP)
[Mk 11:7-9; Ps 118:26]

Mk 10:14 "...for to such belongs the kingdom of God."

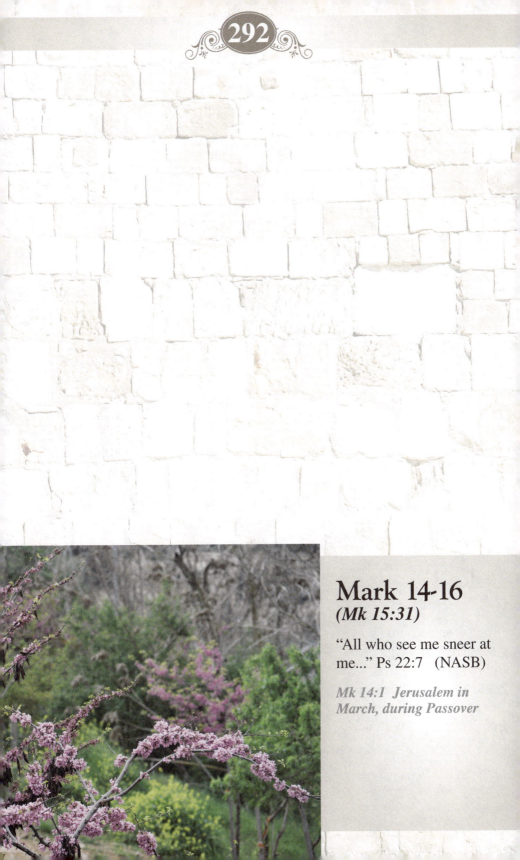

Mark 14-16
(Mk 15:31)

"All who see me sneer at me..." Ps 22:7 (NASB)

Mk 14:1 Jerusalem in March, during Passover

Luke 1-3
(Lk 1:26-37)

"Therefore the Lord Himself shall give you a sign: Behold...a virgin shall conceive and bear a son, and shall call His name Immanuel [God with us]." Isa 7:14 (AMP)

Lk 1:5 Herodium on horizon hilltop, built by Herod; in Judea near Bethlehem

Luke 4-6
(Lk 4:14-21)

"The Spirit of the Lord God is upon me, because the Lord has anointed...me to preach...good tidings..." "...to proclaim liberty..." Is 61:1 (AMP)

Lk 4:1, 2 Gazelle in the Judean Wilderness

Luke 7-9
(Lk 9:17)

(Elisha) "So he set it before them; they ate and left some, as the Lord had said."
2Ki 4:42-44 (AMP)

Lk 9:58 Fox in the Aravah

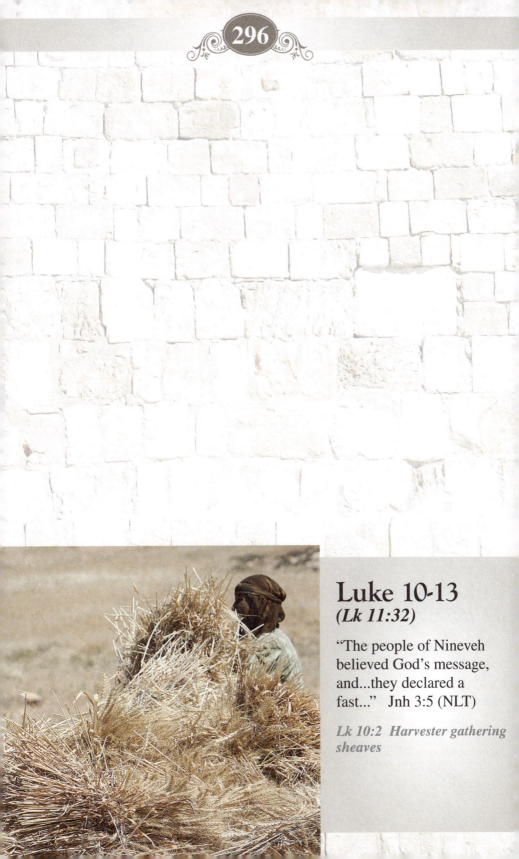

Luke 10-13
(Lk 11:32)

"The people of Nineveh believed God's message, and...they declared a fast..."   Jnh 3:5 (NLT)

Lk 10:2 Harvester gathering sheaves

Luke 14-16
(Lk 16:15)

" 'Man looks at the outward appearance, but the LORD looks at the heart.' "
1Sa 16:7b (NIV)

Lk 15:8 Woman with coin headdress

Luke 17-19
(Lk 17:12-14)

"This shall be the law of the leper on the day when he is to be pronounced clean: he shall be brought to the priest [at a meeting place outside the camp]..." Lv 14:1-32 (AMP)

Lk 18:35 Jericho

Luke 20-22
(Lk 20:41-43)

"The Lord (God) says to my Lord (the Messiah), 'Sit at My right hand...' "
Ps 110:1   (AMP)

Lk 21:37 Olive trees on the Mount of Olives, or "Olivet"

Luke 23-24
(Lk 24:6, 7)

"For You will not abandon my soul to Sheol; Nor will You allow Your Holy One to undergo decay."
Ps 16:10 (NASB)
[Jn 6:69]

John 1-3
(Jn 1:1-3)

"...His name will be called...Mighty God, Eternal Father..."
Is 9:6 (NASB)
[Is 7:14; Jn 8:56-58, 10:30]

John 4-5
(Jn 5:19)

"Moses continued, 'The LORD your God will raise up for you a prophet like me from among your fellow Israelites, You must listen to him.'" Dt 18:15 (NLT) [Jn 5:39, 46, 47]

Jn 4:6 Jacob's well

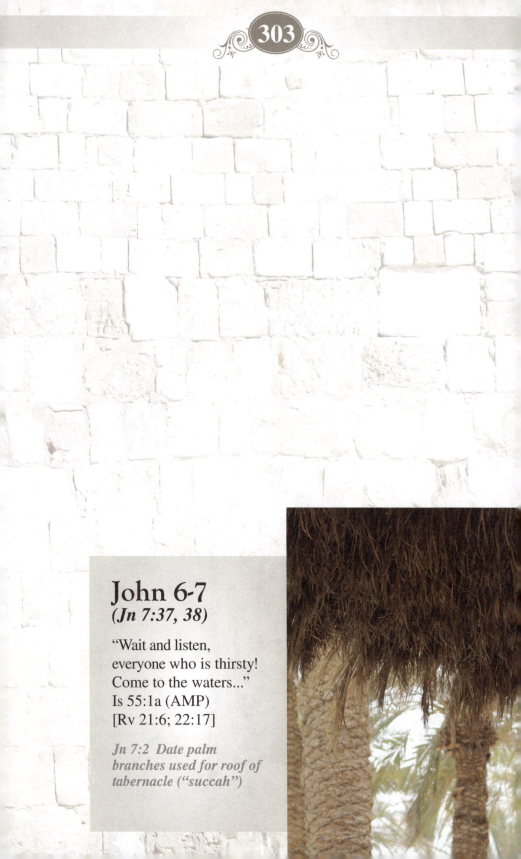

John 6-7
(Jn 7:37, 38)

"Wait and listen, everyone who is thirsty! Come to the waters..."
Is 55:1a (AMP)
[Rv 21:6; 22:17]

Jn 7:2 Date palm branches used for roof of tabernacle ("succah")

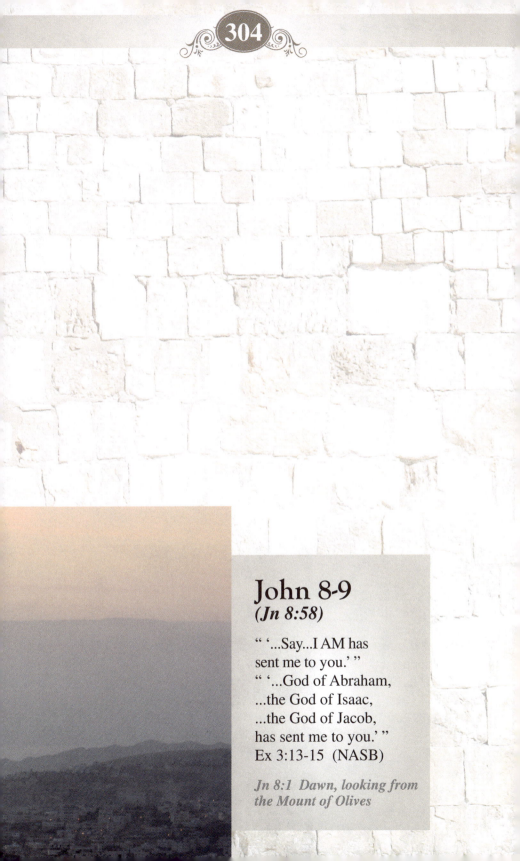

John 8-9
(Jn 8:58)

" '...Say...I AM has sent me to you.' "
" '...God of Abraham, ...the God of Isaac, ...the God of Jacob, has sent me to you.' "
Ex 3:13-15 (NASB)

Jn 8:1 Dawn, looking from the Mount of Olives

John 10-12
(Jn 10:16)

"And I will set over them one shepherd..."
Eze 34:23 (NLT)

Jn 10:9 Sheep going in through the door, "or gate," of the sheepfold

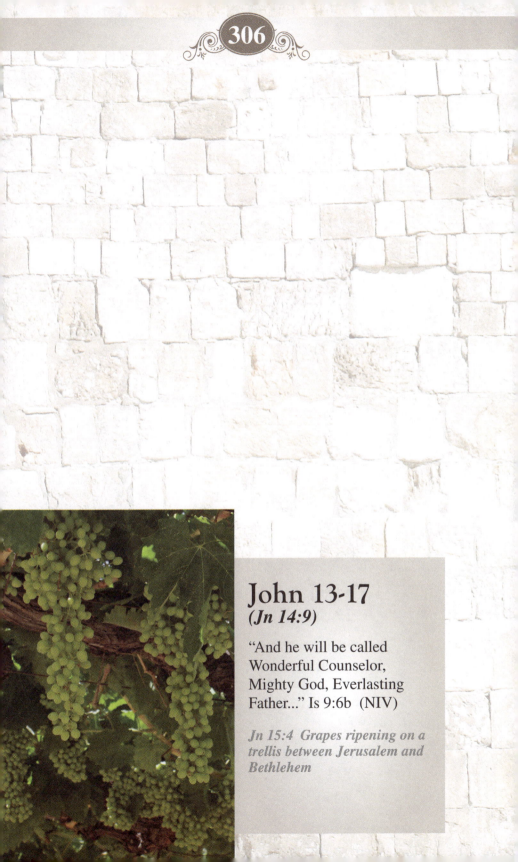

John 13-17
(Jn 14:9)

"And he will be called Wonderful Counselor, Mighty God, Everlasting Father..." Is 9:6b (NIV)

Jn 15:4 Grapes ripening on a trellis between Jerusalem and Bethlehem

John 18-19
(Jn 19:36, 37)

"And they shall look [earnestly] upon Me Whom they have pierced..." Zech 12:10 (AMP) [Rv 1:7]

Jn 18:1 Garden of Gethsemane

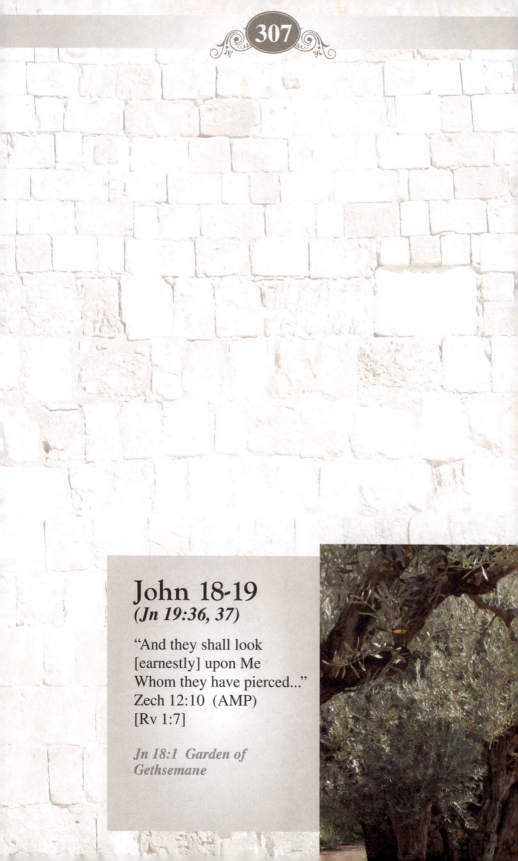

John 20-21
(Jn 20:27, 28)

"For You will not abandon me to Sheol (the place of the dead), neither will You suffer Your holy one [Holy One] to see corruption." Ps 16:10 (AMP)

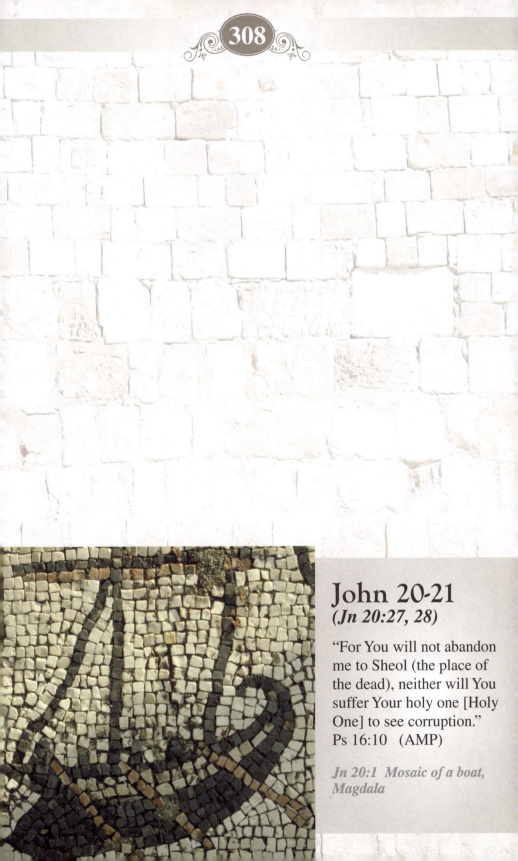

Jn 20:1 Mosaic of a boat, Magdala

Acts 1-3
(Ac 2:5-21, 32, 33)

"And it will come about after this that I will pour out My Spirit on all mankind..."
Joel 2:28, 29 (NASB)
[Ac 2:34, 35; Ps 110:1]

Acts 4-6
(Ac 4:8-12)

"The stone that the builders rejected has now become the cornerstone. This is the LORD's doing..."
Ps 118:22, 23 (NLT)
[Mt 21:42]

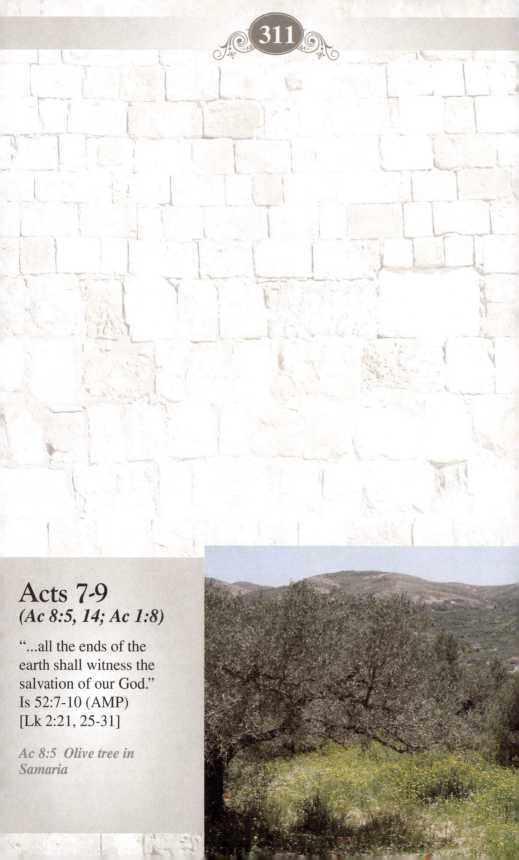

Acts 7-9
(Ac 8:5, 14; Ac 1:8)

"...all the ends of the earth shall witness the salvation of our God."
Is 52:7-10 (AMP)
[Lk 2:21, 25-31]

Ac 8:5 Olive tree in Samaria

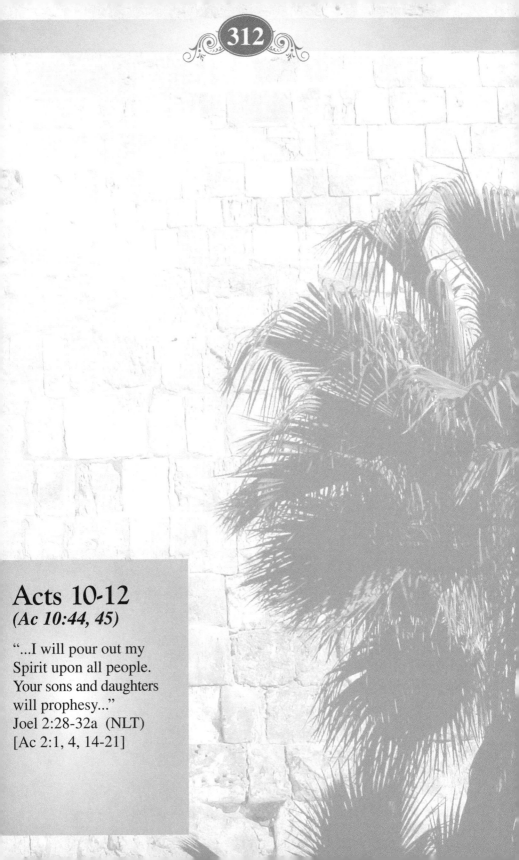

Acts 10-12
(Ac 10:44, 45)

"...I will pour out my Spirit upon all people. Your sons and daughters will prophesy..."
Joel 2:28-32a (NLT)
[Ac 2:1, 4, 14-21]

Acts 13-14
(Ac 13:32-34)

"I will make an everlasting covenant with you, my faithful love promised to David."   Isa 55:3 (NIV) [Ps 2:7; Ps 16:10]

Ac 13:22 Agricultural fields near Bethlehem home of David, son of Jesse

Acts 15
(Ac 15:14-17)

Ac 15:14 "...by taking from the Gentiles a people for himself."
"...'I will restore David's fallen tent...restore its ruins...so that they may possess the remnant...'"
Amos 9:11, 12 (NIV)
[Ac 15:7-9]

James
(Jas 4:12)

"Therefore will I rescue My flock, and they shall no more be a prey; and I will judge between sheep and sheep."
Eze 34:22 (AMP)

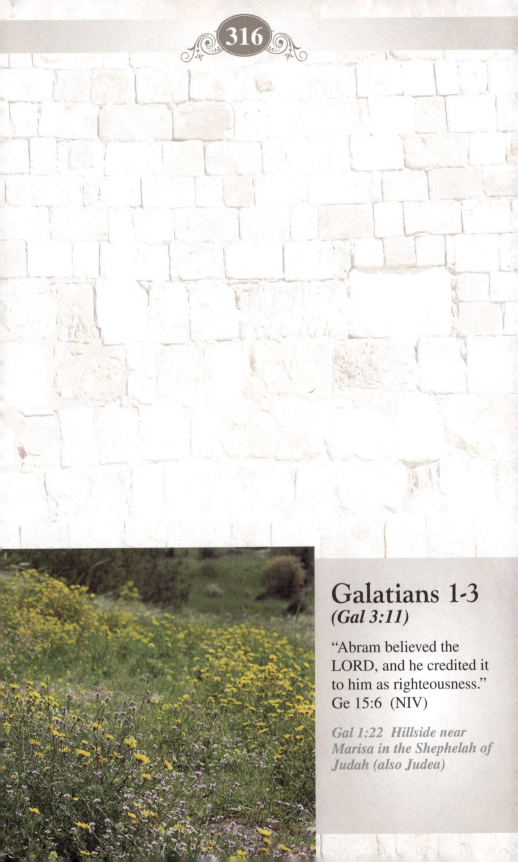

Galatians 1-3
(Gal 3:11)

"Abram believed the LORD, and he credited it to him as righteousness." Ge 15:6 (NIV)

Gal 1:22 Hillside near Marisa in the Shephelah of Judah (also Judea)

Galatians 4-6
(Gal 6:15)

"And the Lord your God will circumcise your hearts and the hearts of your descendants..."
Dt 30:6 [Eze 36:26] (AMP)

Gal 4:1 "...as long as the heir is a child..." (NASB)

Acts 16-18
(Ac 17:31)

"I saw...One like a Son of man..."
"And there was given Him [the Messiah] dominion and glory and kingdom..."
Da 7:13, 14 (AMP)

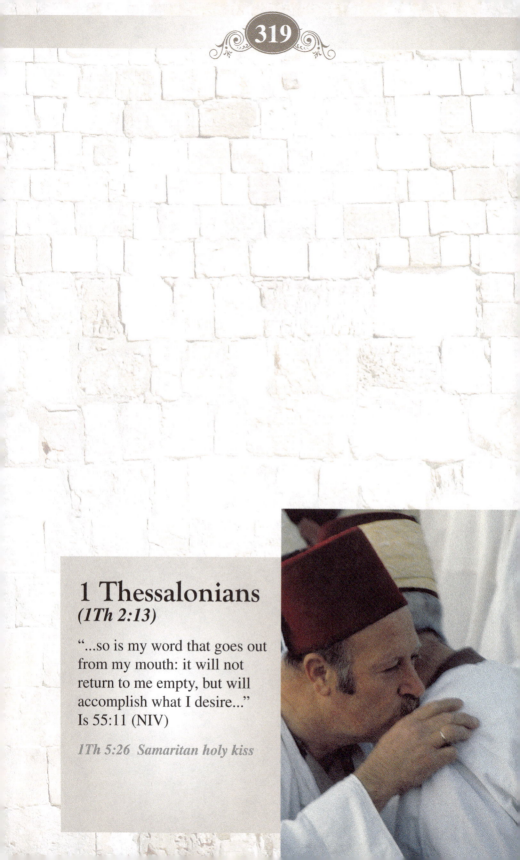

1 Thessalonians
(1Th 2:13)

"...so is my word that goes out from my mouth: it will not return to me empty, but will accomplish what I desire..."
Is 55:11 (NIV)

1Th 5:26 Samaritan holy kiss

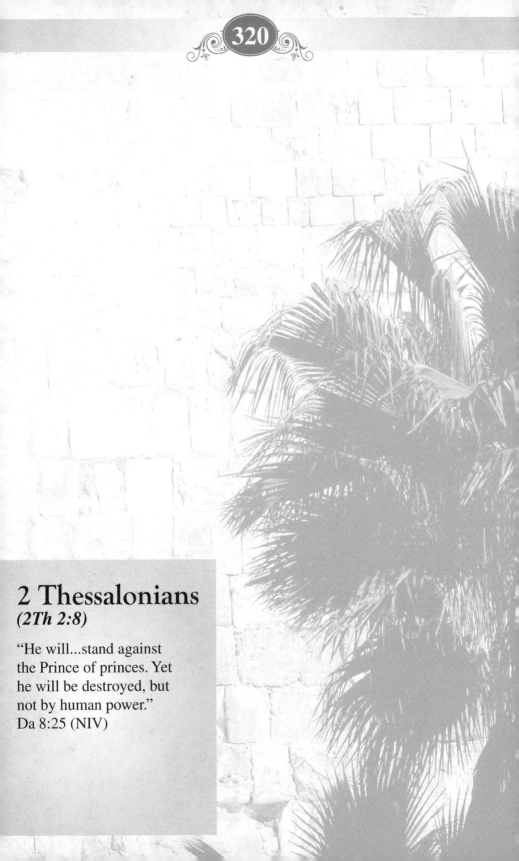

2 Thessalonians
(2Th 2:8)

"He will...stand against the Prince of princes. Yet he will be destroyed, but not by human power."
Da 8:25 (NIV)

1 Corinthians 1-5
(1Cor 1:30)

"...the Spirit of the Lord shall rest upon Him – the Spirit of wisdom..." Isa 11:2a (AMP) [Jer 9:23, 24]

1Co 3:9 Field between Bethlehem and Jerusalem

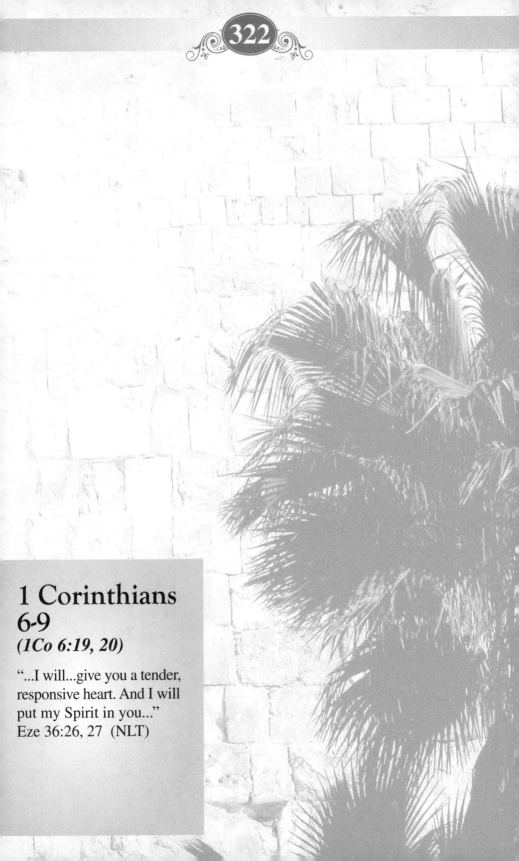

1 Corinthians 6-9
(1Co 6:19, 20)

"...I will...give you a tender, responsive heart. And I will put my Spirit in you..."
Eze 36:26, 27 (NLT)

1 Corinthians 10-11
(1Cor 10:1-4)

"...give the congregation and their livestock drink." Nu 20:1-8; "He brought streams also out of the rock [at Rephidim and Kadesh]..." Ps 78:15, 16 (AMP) [Jn 4:7-14; 7:2, 37, 38; Is 58:11]

324

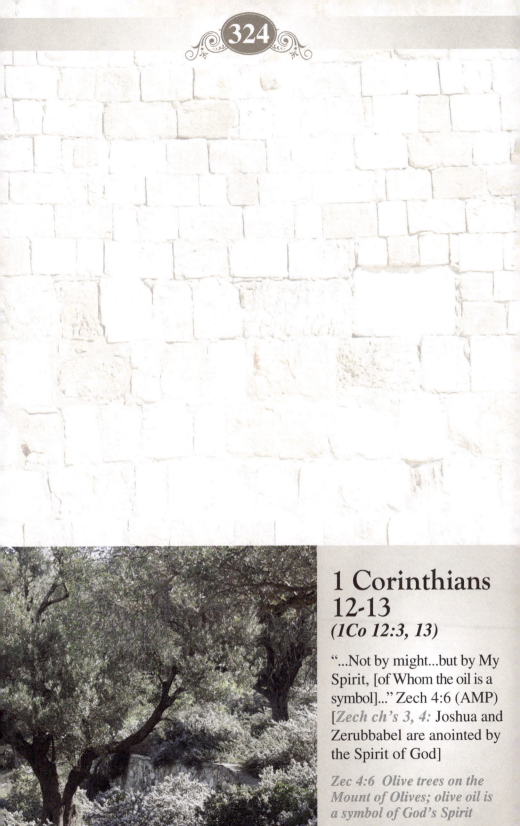

1 Corinthians 12-13
(1Co 12:3, 13)

"...Not by might...but by My Spirit, [of Whom the oil is a symbol]..." Zech 4:6 (AMP) [*Zech ch's 3, 4:* Joshua and Zerubbabel are anointed by the Spirit of God]

Zec 4:6 Olive trees on the Mount of Olives; olive oil is a symbol of God's Spirit

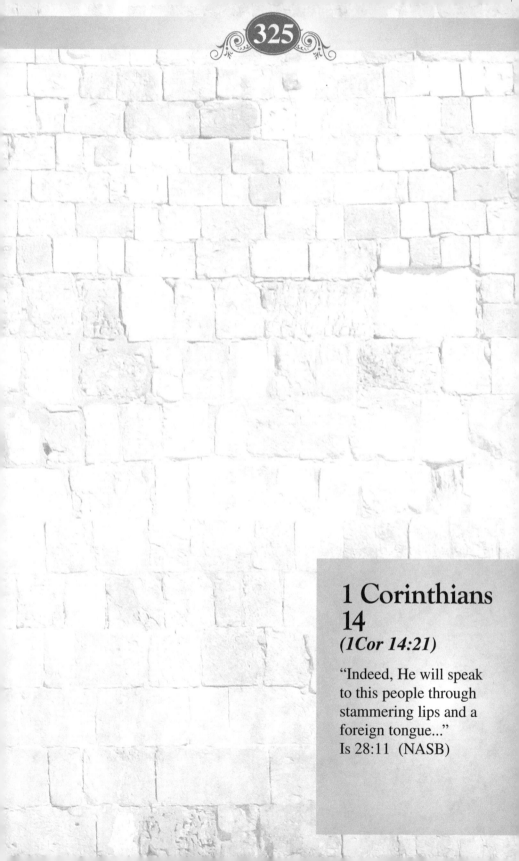

1 Corinthians 14
(1Cor 14:21)

"Indeed, He will speak to this people through stammering lips and a foreign tongue..."
Is 28:11 (NASB)

1 Corinthians 15-16
(1Co 15:24, 25)

"The LORD said to my Lord, 'Sit in the place of honor at My right hand...'"
Ps 110:1 (NLT)
[Is 25:8; Rv 21:3, 4]

2 Corinthians 1-3
(2Co 3:3)

"I will put My law within them, and on their hearts I will write it..." Jer 31:33 [Ex 32:16; Heb 8:8-10] (AMP)

2Co 2:15a "...a sweet fragrance..." Grant-Duff Iris in the Golan

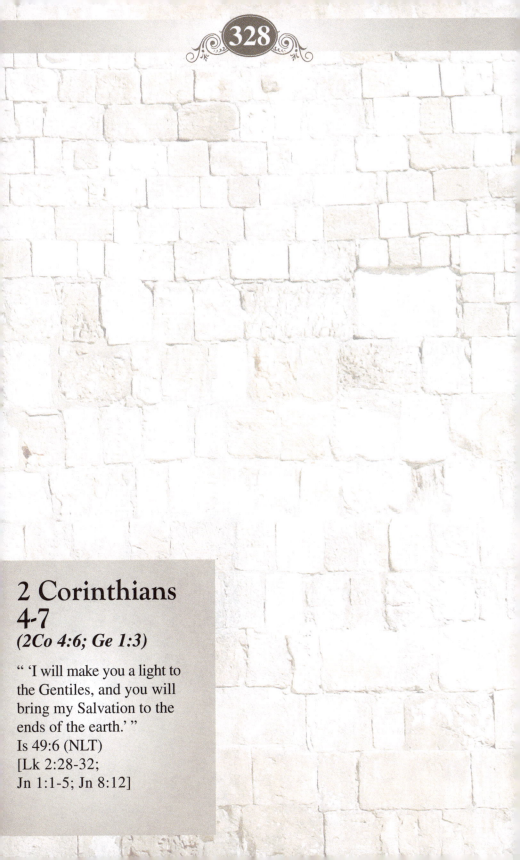

2 Corinthians 4-7
(2Co 4:6; Ge 1:3)

" 'I will make you a light to the Gentiles, and you will bring my Salvation to the ends of the earth.' "
Is 49:6 (NLT)
[Lk 2:28-32; Jn 1:1-5; Jn 8:12]

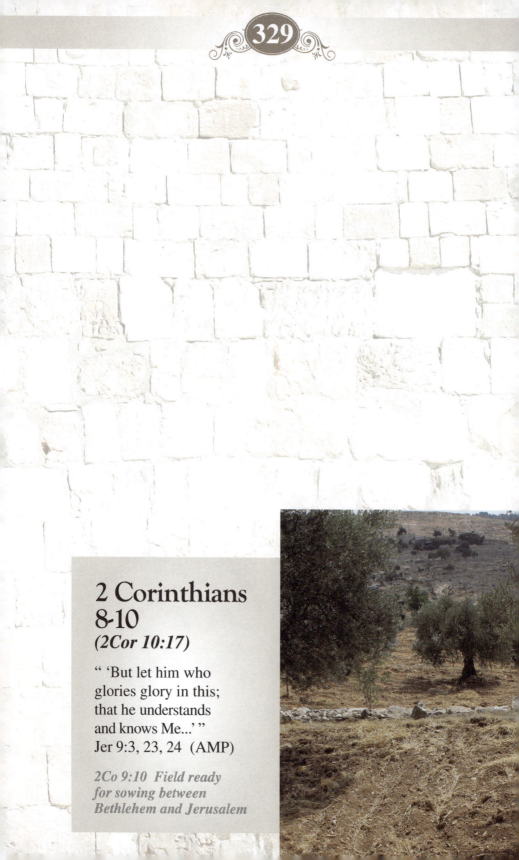

2 Corinthians 8-10
(2Cor 10:17)

" 'But let him who glories glory in this; that he understands and knows Me...' "
Jer 9:3, 23, 24 (AMP)

2Co 9:10 Field ready for sowing between Bethlehem and Jerusalem

2 Corinthians 11-13
(2Cor 11:2)

"And I will even betroth you to Me in stability and in faithfulness, and you shall know...the Lord." Hos 2:16-20 (AMP)

Acts 19-20
(Ac 19:1-4)

"See, I will send my messenger, who will prepare the way before me. Then suddenly the Lord you are seeking will come to his temple..."
Mal 3:1 (NIV)

Ac 19:1 Sea waves at Kushidasi near Ephesus

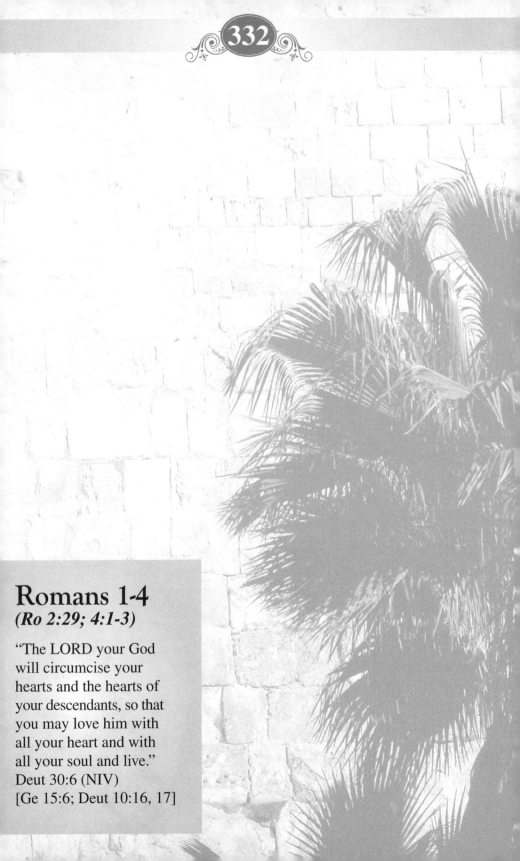

Romans 1-4
(Ro 2:29; 4:1-3)

"The LORD your God will circumcise your hearts and the hearts of your descendants, so that you may love him with all your heart and with all your soul and live."
Deut 30:6 (NIV)
[Ge 15:6; Deut 10:16, 17]

Romans 5-8
(Ro 5:5)

" '...And I will put my Spirit within you...' "
Eze 36:24-27 (AMP)

Ro 7:2 Happy couple

Romans 9-12
(Ro 10:14-15)

"How beautiful upon the mountains are the feet of him who brings good tidings..." Is 52:7 (AMP)

Ro 9:20 Pottery at Qatzrin

Romans 13-16
(Ro 15:8-12)

"...the Root of Jesse will stand as a banner for the peoples; the nations will rally to him and his place of rest will be glorious."
Is 11:10 (NIV)

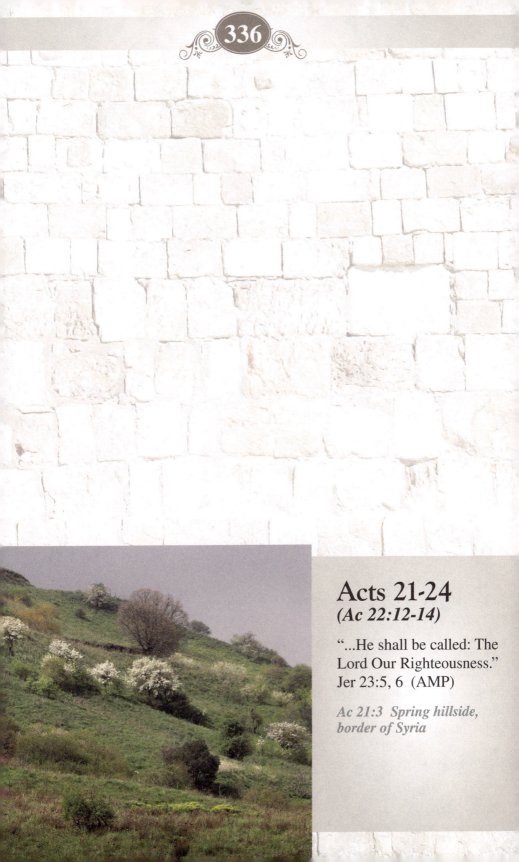

Acts 21-24
(Ac 22:12-14)

"...He shall be called: The Lord Our Righteousness." Jer 23:5, 6 (AMP)

Ac 21:3 Spring hillside, border of Syria

Acts 25-26
(Ac 26:1-3, 13-18, 22, 23; Ro 15:20, 21)

About Messiah: "...So will he sprinkle many nations, and kings will shut their mouths..." "...what they were not told they will see..." Is 52:15 (NIV) [Heb 9:11-15; 10:19-23]

Ac 26:20 Jerusalem, in the region of Judea; looking east from the Mount of Olives

Acts 27-28
(Ac 28:28)

"...that your ways may be known on earth, your salvation among all nations."
Ps 67:1, 2 (NIV)
[Is 49:6]

Ephesians 1-3
(Eph 2:13-18)

"Peace, peace, to him who is far off [both Jew and Gentile] and to him who is near." Isa 57:18, 19 (AMP) [Jn 10:14-17]

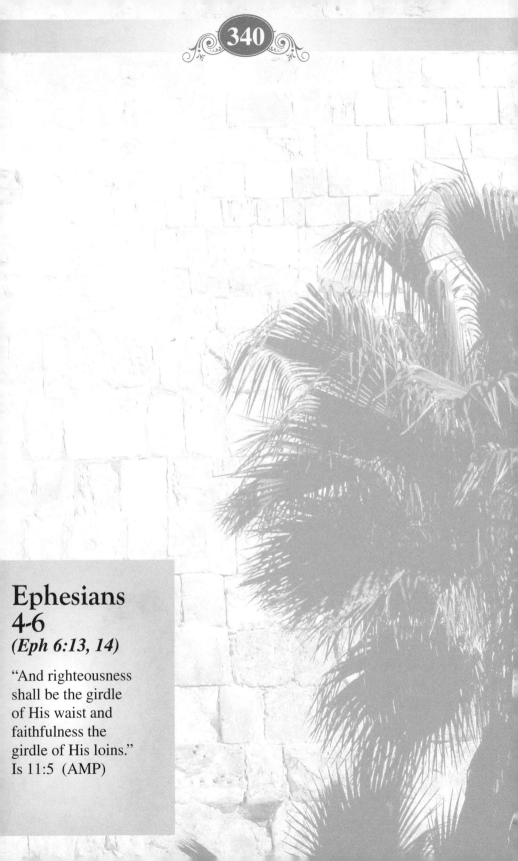

Ephesians 4-6
(Eph 6:13, 14)

"And righteousness shall be the girdle of His waist and faithfulness the girdle of His loins." Is 11:5 (AMP)

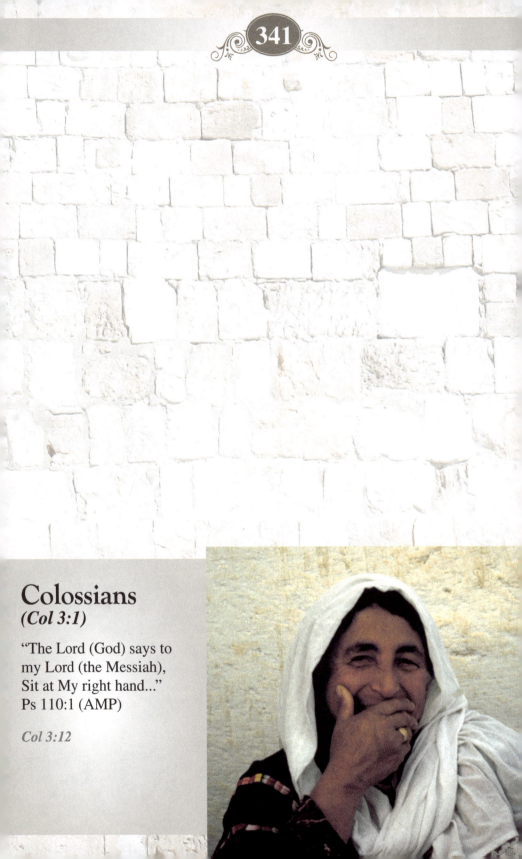

Colossians
(Col 3:1)

"The Lord (God) says to my Lord (the Messiah), Sit at My right hand..."
Ps 110:1 (AMP)

Col 3:12

Philemon - Philippians 1
(Php 1:6)

"The Lord will perfect that which concerns me..."
Ps 138:8 (AMP)

Philippians 2-4
(Php 2:9, 10)

"The government will rest on his shoulders. And he will be called: Wonderful, Counselor, Mighty God, Everlasting Father..."
Is 9:6, 7 (NLT)

Php 2:2 Working together for the harvest

Titus - 1 Peter 1
(1Pe 1:23-25)

"The grass withers and the flowers fade, but the word of our God stands forever."
Is 40:6-9 (NLT)

1 Peter 2-5
(1Pe 2:4-7; Ps 118:22)

"...I am laying in Zion for a foundation Stone, a tested Stone, a precious Cornerstone of sure foundation..."
Is 28:16 (AMP)
[Eph 2:19-22]

1Pe 2:25 Sheep and lambs between Jericho and the Dead Sea

1 Timothy 1-3
(1Ti 2:1-4)

" 'Turn to me and be saved, all you ends of the earth: for I am God, and there is no other...' "
Is 45:18-23 (NIV)

1 Timothy 4-6
(1Ti 6:13-15)

Keeping His precepts:
Mt 28:18-20
"His dominion is an everlasting dominion... which shall not be destroyed."
Da 7:14 (AMP)

Messiah's good confession: Jn 18:36, 37

2 Peter
(2Pe 3:13)

"For behold, I create new heavens and a new earth..."
Is 65:17, 18 (AMP)
[Rv 21:1]

2Pe 1:19 Olive oil lamp at Qatzrin

2 Timothy
(2Ti 2:8)

David prays: "...'may it please You to bless the house of Your servant, that it may continue forever before You...' " 2Sa 7:29 (NASB) [Is 11:1; Micah 5:2; Mt 1:6, 20-25; 20:29-34]

2Ti 1:6 Fanning the flame "..kindle afresh..."

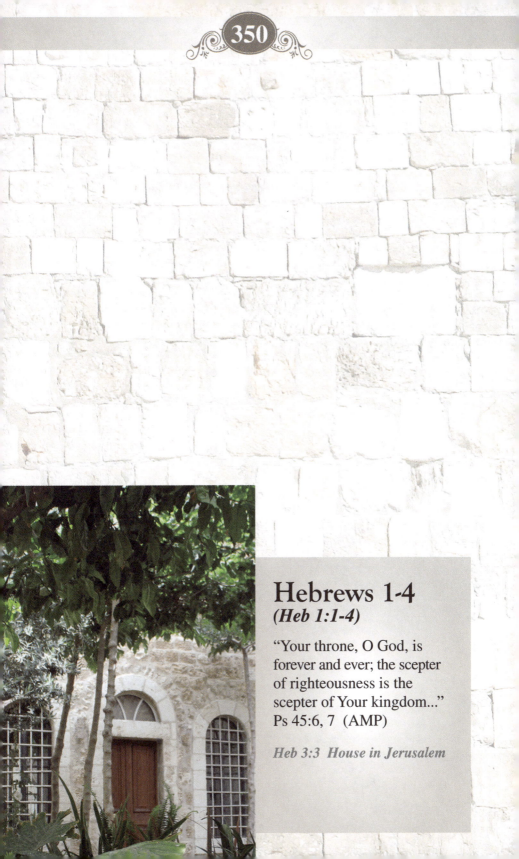

Hebrews 1-4
(Heb 1:1-4)

"Your throne, O God, is forever and ever; the scepter of righteousness is the scepter of Your kingdom..."
Ps 45:6, 7 (AMP)

Heb 3:3 House in Jerusalem

Hebrews 5-8
(Heb 7:23, 24)

" 'You are a priest forever in the order of Melchizedek.' "
Ps 110:4 (NLT)

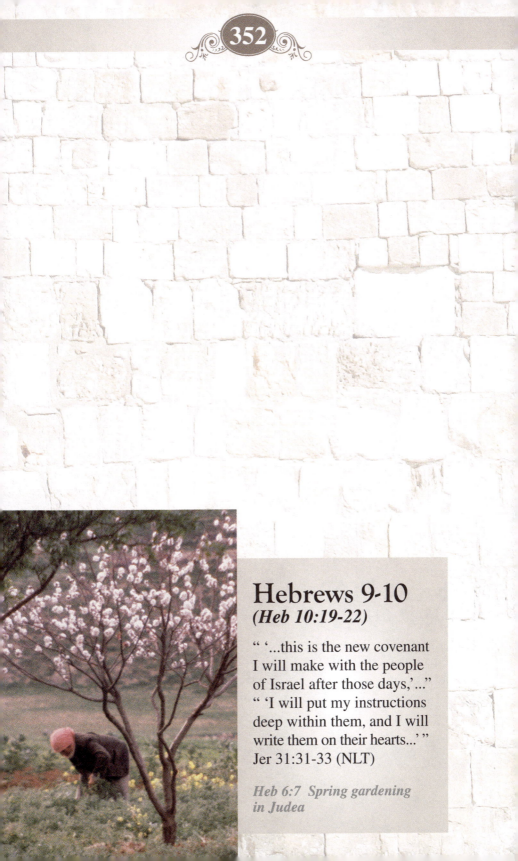

Hebrews 9-10
(Heb 10:19-22)

" '...this is the new covenant I will make with the people of Israel after those days,'..." " 'I will put my instructions deep within them, and I will write them on their hearts...' " Jer 31:31-33 (NLT)

Heb 6:7 Spring gardening in Judea

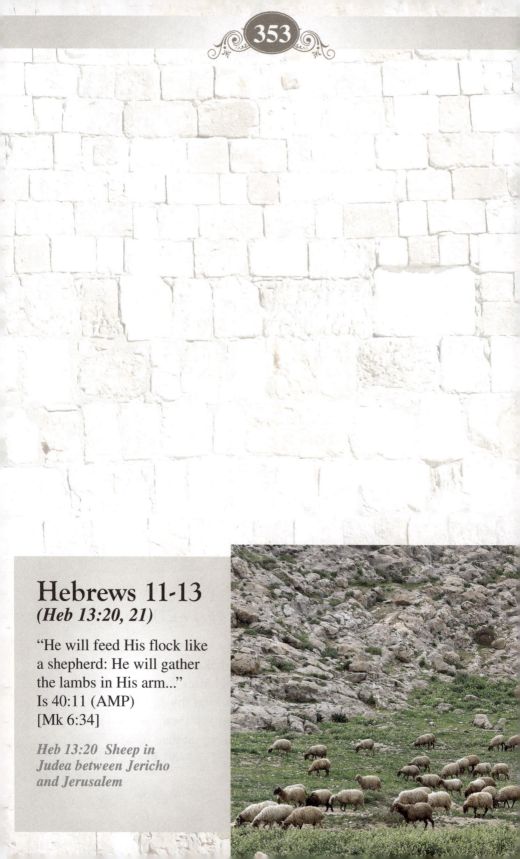

Hebrews 11-13
(Heb 13:20, 21)

"He will feed His flock like a shepherd: He will gather the lambs in His arm..."
Is 40:11 (AMP)
[Mk 6:34]

Heb 13:20 Sheep in Judea between Jericho and Jerusalem

Jude - 1 John 1-2
(1Jn 2:23-25)

"...to us a son is given..."
"...And he will be called...
Mighty God, Everlasting
Father..." Is 9:6 (NIV)

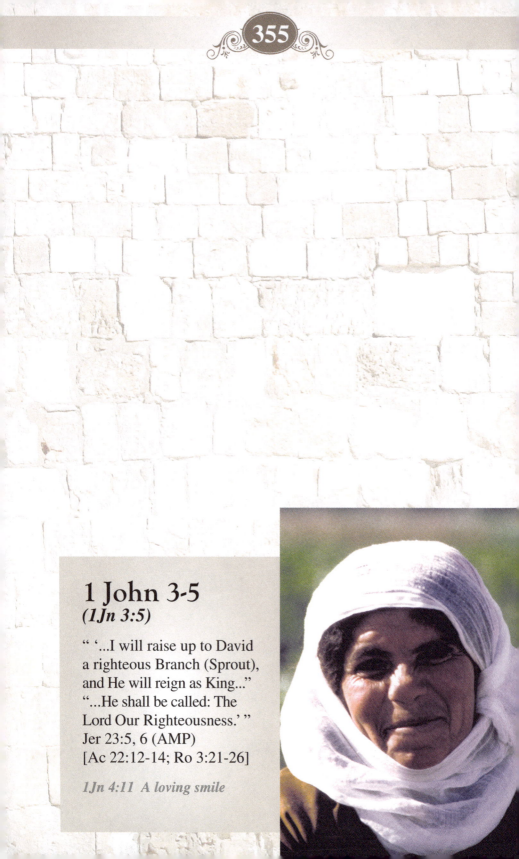

1 John 3-5
(1Jn 3:5)

" '...I will raise up to David a righteous Branch (Sprout), and He will reign as King...' "
"...He shall be called: The Lord Our Righteousness.' "
Jer 23:5, 6 (AMP)
[Ac 22:12-14; Ro 3:21-26]

1Jn 4:11 A loving smile

2 John-
3 John
(3Jn vs 7)

"...and shall call his name Immanuel [God with us]."
Is 7:14 (AMP)

Revelation 1-3
(Rv 1:7)

"They will look on me, the one they have pierced, and they will mourn..."
Zech 12:10 (NIV)
[Jn 19:30, 33-37]

Rv 1:14 Jerusalem snow

Revelation 4-6
(Rv 5:1-5)

"He...crouched like a lion... who dares provoke and rouse him?..." "The scepter...shall not depart from Judah..."
Ge 49:9, 10 (AMP)

The Lion: Hos 11:1-3, 8, 10;
The Lamb: Is 53:7; Rv 5:6, 9

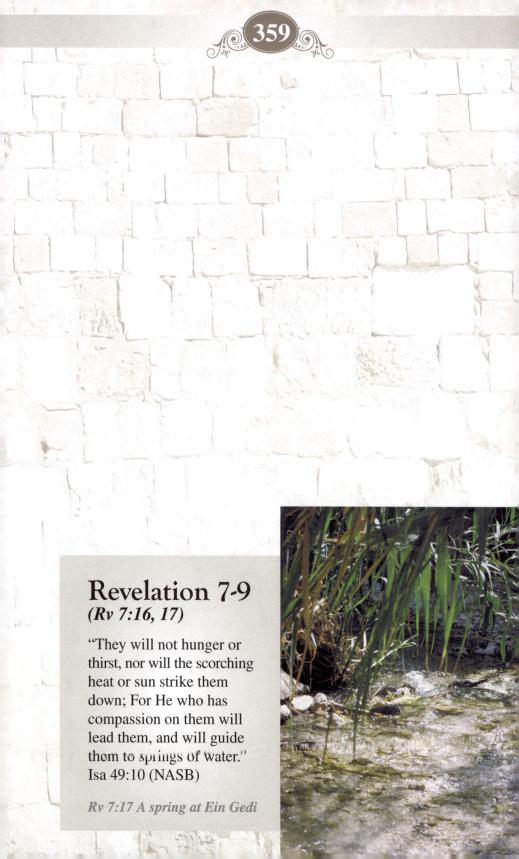

Revelation 7-9
(Rv 7:16, 17)

"They will not hunger or thirst, nor will the scorching heat or sun strike them down; For He who has compassion on them will lead them, and will guide them to springs of water."
Isa 49:10 (NASB)

Rv 7:17 A spring at Ein Gedi

Revelation 10-12
(Rv 12:5)

"The Lord (God) says to my Lord (the Messiah), Sit at My right hand, until I make Your Adversaries Your footstool."
Ps 110:1, 2 (AMP)

Revelation 13-15
(Rv 15:8)

"I looked, and behold, the glory of the Lord filled the house of the Lord, and I fell upon my face."
Eze 40:1-4; 44:4 (AMP)

Revelation 16-18
(Rv 17:12-14)

"...there was given Him [the Messiah] dominion ...that all peoples, nations, and languages should serve Him. His dominion is an everlasting dominion..."
Dan 7:1, 13, 14 (AMP)

Revelation 19-22
(Rv 21:6)

"Come, all you who are thirsty, come to the waters..." Is 55:1 (NIV)

Thirsty: Jn 7:37, 38; Rv 22:17
First and Last: Is 44:6; Rv 1:5, 8, 17; 21:6

Rv 21:6 Spring waters of Ein Gedi

Rev 21:22, 23

"Then the moon will be confounded and the sun ashamed, when [they compare...to the light of] the Lord of hosts..."
Is 24:23 (AMP)

Rv 21:23 "...no need of the sun nor of the moon..."
Moon over the Sea of Galilee near Hippus

Messiah Revealed: The Promise of the Ages Journal is a read through the Bible guide revealing Messianic connections with 250 Holyland photos

*This read through the Bible list may be copied

- [ ] 1 Genesis 1-3
- [ ] 2 Genesis 4-6
- [ ] 3 Genesis 7-9
- [ ] 4 Genesis 10-11
- [ ] 5 Genesis 12-16
- [ ] 6 Genesis 17-20
- [ ] 7 Genesis 21-24:10
- [ ] 8 Genesis 24:11-26:35
- [ ] 9 Genesis 27-29
- [ ] 10 Genesis 30-32:23
- [ ] 11 Genesis 32:24-35:29
- [ ] 12 Genesis 36-39
- [ ] 13 Genesis 40-43
- [ ] 14 Genesis 44-46
- [ ] 15 Genesis 47-50
- [ ] 16 Job 1-4
- [ ] 17 Job 5-7
- [ ] 18 Job 8-10
- [ ] 19 Job 11-13
- [ ] 20 Job 14-17
- [ ] 21 Job 18-20
- [ ] 22 Job 21-24
- [ ] 23 Job 25-28
- [ ] 24 Job 29-31
- [ ] 25 Job 32-34
- [ ] 26 Job 35-38
- [ ] 27 Job 39-42
- [ ] 28 Exodus 1-4
- [ ] 29 Exodus 5-8
- [ ] 30 Exodus 9-11
- [ ] 31 Exodus 12-13
- [ ] 32 Exodus 14-15
- [ ] 33 Exodus 16-18
- [ ] 34 Exodus 19-22
- [ ] 35 Exodus 23-27
- [ ] 36 Exodus 28-29
- [ ] 37 Exodus 30-33
- [ ] 38 Exodus 34-36
- [ ] 39 Exodus 37-40
- [ ] 40 Leviticus 1-4
- [ ] 41 Leviticus 5-7
- [ ] 42 Leviticus 8-9
- [ ] 43 Leviticus 10-13
- [ ] 44 Leviticus 14-16:25
- [ ] 45 Leviticus 16:26-19:11
- [ ] 46 Leviticus 19:12-21:24
- [ ] 47 Leviticus 22-24
- [ ] 48 Leviticus 25-27
- [ ] 49 Numbers 1-5
- [ ] 50 Numbers 6-10
- [ ] 51 Numbers 11-14
- [ ] 52 Numbers 15-17
- [ ] 53 Numbers 18-20
- [ ] 54 Numbers 21-23
- [ ] 55 Numbers 24-27
- [ ] 56 Numbers 28-30
- [ ] 57 Numbers 31-33
- [ ] 58 Numbers 34-36
- [ ] 59 Deuteronomy 1-3
- [ ] 60 Deuteronomy 4-6
- [ ] 61 Deuteronomy 7-9
- [ ] 62 Deuteronomy 10-12
- [ ] 63 Deuteronomy 13-15
- [ ] 64 Deuteronomy 16-17
- [ ] 65 Deuteronomy 18-20
- [ ] 66 Deuteronomy 21-24
- [ ] 67 Deuteronomy 25-28
- [ ] 68 Deuteronomy 29-31
- [ ] 69 Deuteronomy 32-34
- [ ] 70 Joshua 1-3
- [ ] 71 Joshua 4-6
- [ ] 72 Joshua 7-9
- [ ] 73 Joshua 10-12
- [ ] 74 Joshua 13-16
- [ ] 75 Joshua 17-19
- [ ] 76 Joshua 20-22
- [ ] 77 Joshua 23-24
- [ ] 78 Judges 1-4
- [ ] 79 Judges 5-7
- [ ] 80 Judges 8-12
- [ ] 81 Judges 13-16
- [ ] 82 Judges 17-19
- [ ] 83 Judges 20-21
- [ ] 84 Ruth 1-4
- [ ] 85 1 Samuel 1-5
- [ ] 86 1 Samuel 6-8
- [ ] 87 1 Samuel 9-11
- [ ] 88 1 Samuel 12-14
- [ ] 89 1 Samuel 15-18
- [ ] 90 1 Samuel 19-21
- [ ] 91 1 Samuel 22-24
- [ ] 92 1 Samuel 25-28
- [ ] 93 1 Samuel 29-31
- [ ] 94 2 Samuel 1-3
- [ ] 95 2 Samuel 4-7
- [ ] 96 2 Samuel 8-12
- [ ] 97 2 Samuel 13-16
- [ ] 98 2 Samuel 17-18
- [ ] 99 2 Samuel 19-21
- [ ] 100 2 Samuel 22-24
- [ ] 101 1 Kings 1-3
- [ ] 102 Psalms 1-4
- [ ] 103 Psalms 5-7
- [ ] 104 Psalms 8-11
- [ ] 105 Psalms 12-16
- [ ] 106 Psalms 17-20
- [ ] 107 Psalms 21-22
- [ ] 108 Psalms 23-26
- [ ] 109 Psalms 27-31
- [ ] 110 Psalms 32-33
- [ ] 111 Psalms 34
- [ ] 112 Psalms 35-37
- [ ] 113 Psalms 38-40
- [ ] 114 Psalms 41-45
- [ ] 115 Psalms 46-50
- [ ] 116 Psalms 51-55
- [ ] 117 Psalms 56-60
- [ ] 118 Psalms 61-65
- [ ] 119 Psalms 66-68
- [ ] 120 Psalms 69-71
- [ ] 121 Psalms 72-73
- [ ] 122 Psalms 74-77
- [ ] 123 Psalms 78-79
- [ ] 124 Psalms 80-82
- [ ] 125 Psalms 83-87
- [ ] 126 Psalms 88-89
- [ ] 127 Psalms 90-92
- [ ] 128 Psalms 93-97
- [ ] 129 Psalms 98-102
- [ ] 130 Psalms 103
- [ ] 131 Psalms 104-105
- [ ] 132 Psalms 106
- [ ] 133 Psalms 107
- [ ] 134 Psalms 108-109
- [ ] 135 Psalms 110-114
- [ ] 136 Psalms 115-117
- [ ] 137 Psalms 118
- [ ] 138 Psalms 119
- [ ] 139 Psalms 120-130
- [ ] 140 Psalms 131-134
- [ ] 141 Psalms 135-139
- [ ] 142 Psalms 140-143
- [ ] 143 Psalms 144-145
- [ ] 144 Psalms 146
- [ ] 145 Psalms 147
- [ ] 146 Psalms 148-150
- [ ] 147 1 Chronicles 1-3
- [ ] 148 1 Chronicles 4-6
- [ ] 149 1 Chronicles 7-9
- [ ] 150 1 Chronicles 10-12
- [ ] 151 1 Chronicles 13-16
- [ ] 152 1 Chronicles 17-20
- [ ] 153 1 Chronicles 21-22
- [ ] 154 1 Chronicles 23-26
- [ ] 155 1 Chronicles 27-29
- [ ] 156 2 Chronicles 1-3
- [ ] 157 2 Chronicles 4-6
- [ ] 158 2 Chronicles 7-9
- [ ] 159 Song of Solomon 1-3
- [ ] 160 Song of Solomon 4-8
- [ ] 161 Proverbs 1-3
- [ ] 162 Proverbs 4-7
- [ ] 163 Proverbs 8-11
- [ ] 164 Proverbs 12-15
- [ ] 165 Proverbs 16-19
- [ ] 166 Proverbs 20-21
- [ ] 167 Proverbs 22-24
- [ ] 168 Proverbs 25-27
- [ ] 169 Proverbs 28-29
- [ ] 170 Proverbs 30-31
- [ ] 171 Ecclesiastes 1-6
- [ ] 172 Ecclesiastes 7-12
- [ ] 173 1 Kings 4-7
- [ ] 174 1 Kings 8-9
- [ ] 175 1 Kings 10-11

☐	176	1 Kings 12-15	☐	239	Jeremiah 31-32	☐	302	John 4-5
☐	177	1 Kings 16-18	☐	240	Jeremiah 33-36	☐	303	John 6-7
☐	178	1 Kings 19-22	☐	241	Jeremiah 37-40	☐	304	John 8-9
☐	179	2 Chronicles 10-13	☐	242	Jeremiah 41-43	☐	305	John 10-12
☐	180	2 Chronicles 14-16	☐	243	Jeremiah 44-48	☐	306	John 13-17
☐	181	2 Chronicles 17-18	☐	244	Jeremiah 49	☐	307	John 18-19
☐	182	2 Kings 1-3	☐	245	Jeremiah 50	☐	308	John 20-21
☐	183	2 Chronicles 19-21	☐	246	Jeremiah 51-52	☐	309	Acts 1-3
☐	184	2 Kings 4-6	☐	247	Lamentations	☐	310	Acts 4-6
☐	185	2 Kings 7-10	☐	248	Ezekiel 1-3	☐	311	Acts 7-9
☐	186	Joel	☐	249	Ezekiel 4-7	☐	312	Acts 10-12
☐	187	2 Chronicles 22-25	☐	250	Ezekiel 8-10	☐	313	Acts 13-14
☐	188	2 Kings 11-14	☐	251	Ezekiel 11-15	☐	314	Acts 15
☐	189	Jonah	☐	252	Ezekiel 16-17	☐	315	James
☐	190	Amos 1-3	☐	253	Ezekiel 18-21	☐	316	Galatians 1-3
☐	191	Amos 4-6	☐	254	Ezekiel 22-24	☐	317	Galatians 4-6
☐	192	Amos 7-9	☐	255	Ezekiel 25-28	☐	318	Acts 16-18
☐	193	2 Chronicles 26-29	☐	256	Ezekiel 29-31	☐	319	1 Thessalonians
☐	194	2 Kings 15-17	☐	257	Ezekiel 32-33	☐	320	2 Thessalonians
☐	195	2 Kings 18-20	☐	258	Ezekiel 34-36	☐	321	1 Corinthians 1-5
☐	196	2 Chronicles 30-32	☐	259	Ezekiel 37-39	☐	322	1 Corinthians 6-9
☐	197	Isaiah 36-39	☐	260	Ezekiel 40-42	☐	323	1 Corinthians 10-11
☐	198	2 Kings 21	☐	261	Ezekiel 43-45	☐	324	1 Corinthians 12-13
☐	199	Hosea 1-4	☐	262	Ezekiel 46-48	☐	325	1 Corinthians 14
☐	200	Hosea 5-9	☐	263	Daniel 1-3	☐	326	1 Corinthians 15-16
☐	201	Hosea 10-14	☐	264	Daniel 4-6	☐	327	2 Corinthians 1-3
☐	202	Micah 1-4	☐	265	Daniel 7-9	☐	328	2 Corinthians 4-7
☐	203	Micah 5-7	☐	266	Daniel 10-12	☐	329	2 Corinthians 8-10
☐	204	Isaiah 1-3	☐	267	Ezra 1-5	☐	330	2 Corinthians 11-13
☐	205	Isaiah 4-6	☐	268	Haggai	☐	331	Acts 19-20
☐	206	Isaiah 7-8	☐	269	Zechariah 1-5	☐	332	Romans 1-4
☐	207	Isaiah 9-10	☐	270	Zechariah 6-9	☐	333	Romans 5-8
☐	208	Isaiah 11-15	☐	271	Zechariah 10-14	☐	334	Romans 9-12
☐	209	Isaiah 16-18	☐	272	Ezra 6-10	☐	335	Romans 13-16
☐	210	Isaiah 19-22	☐	273	Nehemiah 1-4	☐	336	Acts 21-24
☐	211	Isaiah 23-26	☐	274	Nehemiah 5-8	☐	337	Acts 25-26
☐	212	Isaiah 27-29	☐	275	Nehemiah 9-10	☐	338	Acts 27-28
☐	213	Isaiah 30-33	☐	276	Nehemiah 11-13	☐	339	Ephesians 1-3
☐	214	Isaiah 34-35	☐	277	Esther 1-6	☐	340	Ephesians 4-6
☐	215	Isaiah 40-41	☐	278	Esther 7-10	☐	341	Colossians
☐	216	Isaiah 42-43	☐	279	Malachi	☐	342	Philemon- Philip.1
☐	217	Isaiah 44-48	☐	280	Matthew 1-3	☐	343	Philippians 2-4
☐	218	Isaiah 49-51	☐	281	Matthew 4-8	☐	344	Titus - 1 Peter 1
☐	219	Isaiah 52-54	☐	282	Matthew 9-11	☐	345	1 Peter 2-5
☐	220	Isaiah 55-58	☐	283	Matthew 12-13	☐	346	1 Timothy 1-3
☐	221	Isaiah 59-60	☐	284	Matthew 14-16	☐	347	1 Timothy 4-6
☐	222	Isaiah 61-64	☐	285	Matthew 17-20	☐	348	2 Peter
☐	223	Isaiah 65-66	☐	286	Matthew 21-24	☐	349	2 Timothy
☐	224	Nahum	☐	287	Matthew 25-28	☐	350	Hebrews 1-4
☐	225	Zephaniah	☐	288	Mark 1-3	☐	351	Hebrews 5-8
☐	226	Habakkuk	☐	289	Mark 4-5	☐	352	Hebrews 9-10
☐	227	Obadiah	☐	290	Mark 6-9	☐	353	Hebrews 11-13
☐	228	2 Kings 22-25	☐	291	Mark 10-13	☐	354	Jude - 1 John 1-2
☐	229	2 Chronicles 33-36	☐	292	Mark 14-16	☐	355	1 John 3-5
☐	230	Jeremiah 1-3	☐	293	Luke 1-3	☐	356	2 John - 3 John
☐	231	Jeremiah 4-5	☐	294	Luke 4-6	☐	357	Revelation 1-3
☐	232	Jeremiah 6-8	☐	295	Luke 7-9	☐	358	Revelation 4-6
☐	233	Jeremiah 9-12	☐	296	Luke 10-13	☐	359	Revelation 7-9
☐	234	Jeremiah 13-16	☐	297	Luke 14-16	☐	360	Revelation 10-12
☐	235	Jeremiah 17-20	☐	298	Luke 17-19	☐	361	Revelation 13-15
☐	236	Jeremiah 21-24	☐	299	Luke 20-22	☐	362	Revelation 16-18
☐	237	Jeremiah 25-27	☐	300	Luke 23-24	☐	363	Revelation 19-22
☐	238	Jeremiah 28-30	☐	301	John 1-3			

<u>**Messiah Revealed: The Promise of the Ages Journal**</u> is a read through the Bible guide revealing Messianic connections with 250 Holyland photos

This read through the Bible list may be copied

- 1 Genesis 1-3
- 2 Genesis 4-6
- 3 Genesis 7-9
- 4 Genesis 10-11
- 5 Genesis 12-16
- 6 Genesis 17-20
- 7 Genesis 21-24:10
- 8 Genesis 24:11-26:35
- 9 Genesis 27-29
- 10 Genesis 30-32:23
- 11 Genesis 32:24-35:29
- 12 Genesis 36-39
- 13 Genesis 40-43
- 14 Genesis 44-46
- 15 Genesis 47-50
- 16 Job 1-4
- 17 Job 5-7
- 18 Job 8-10
- 19 Job 11-13
- 20 Job 14-17
- 21 Job 18-20
- 22 Job 21-24
- 23 Job 25-28
- 24 Job 29-31
- 25 Job 32-34
- 26 Job 35-38
- 27 Job 39-42
- 28 Exodus 1-4
- 29 Exodus 5-8
- 30 Exodus 9-11
- 31 Exodus 12-13
- 32 Exodus 14-15
- 33 Exodus 16-18
- 34 Exodus 19-22
- 35 Exodus 23-27
- 36 Exodus 28-29
- 37 Exodus 30-33
- 38 Exodus 34-36
- 39 Exodus 37-40
- 40 Leviticus 1-4
- 41 Leviticus 5-7
- 42 Leviticus 8-9
- 43 Leviticus 10-13
- 44 Leviticus 14-16:25
- 45 Leviticus 16:26-19:11
- 46 Leviticus 19:12-21:24
- 47 Leviticus 22-24
- 48 Leviticus 25-27
- 49 Numbers 1-5
- 50 Numbers 6-10
- 51 Numbers 11-14
- 52 Numbers 15-17
- 53 Numbers 18-20
- 54 Numbers 21-23
- 55 Numbers 24-27
- 56 Numbers 28-30
- 57 Numbers 31-33
- 58 Numbers 34-36
- 59 Deuteronomy 1-3
- 60 Deuteronomy 4-6
- 61 Deuteronomy 7-9
- 62 Deuteronomy 10-12
- 63 Deuteronomy 13-15
- 64 Deuteronomy 16-17
- 65 Deuteronomy 18-20
- 66 Deuteronomy 21-24
- 67 Deuteronomy 25-28
- 68 Deuteronomy 29-31
- 69 Deuteronomy 32-34
- 70 Joshua 1-3
- 71 Joshua 4-6
- 72 Joshua 7-9
- 73 Joshua 10-12
- 74 Joshua 13-16
- 75 Joshua 17-19
- 76 Joshua 20-22
- 77 Joshua 23-24
- 78 Judges 1-4
- 79 Judges 5-7
- 80 Judges 8-12
- 81 Judges 13-16
- 82 Judges 17-19
- 83 Judges 20-21
- 84 Ruth 1-4
- 85 1 Samuel 1-5
- 86 1 Samuel 6-8
- 87 1 Samuel 9-11
- 88 1 Samuel 12-14
- 89 1 Samuel 15-18
- 90 1 Samuel 19-21
- 91 1 Samuel 22-24
- 92 1 Samuel 25-28
- 93 1 Samuel 29-31
- 94 2 Samuel 1-3
- 95 2 Samuel 4-7
- 96 2 Samuel 8-12
- 97 2 Samuel 13-16
- 98 2 Samuel 17-18
- 99 2 Samuel 19-21
- 100 2 Samuel 22-24
- 101 1 Kings 1-3
- 102 Psalms 1-4
- 103 Psalms 5-7
- 104 Psalms 8-11
- 105 Psalms 12-16
- 106 Psalms 17-20
- 107 Psalms 21-22
- 108 Psalms 23-26
- 109 Psalms 27-31
- 110 Psalms 32-33
- 111 Psalms 34
- 112 Psalms 35-37
- 113 Psalms 38-40
- 114 Psalms 41-45
- 115 Psalms 46-50
- 116 Psalms 51-55
- 117 Psalms 56-60
- 118 Psalms 61-65
- 119 Psalms 66-68
- 120 Psalms 69-71
- 121 Psalms 72-73
- 122 Psalms 74-77
- 123 Psalms 78-79
- 124 Psalms 80-82
- 125 Psalms 83-87
- 126 Psalms 88-89
- 127 Psalms 90-92
- 128 Psalms 93-97
- 129 Psalms 98-102
- 130 Psalms 103
- 131 Psalms 104-105
- 132 Psalms 106
- 133 Psalms 107
- 134 Psalms 108-109
- 135 Psalms 110-114
- 136 Psalms 115-117
- 137 Psalms 118
- 138 Psalms 119
- 139 Psalms 120-130
- 140 Psalms 131-134
- 141 Psalms 135-139
- 142 Psalms 140-143
- 143 Psalms 144-145
- 144 Psalms 146
- 145 Psalms 147
- 146 Psalms 148-150
- 147 1 Chronicles 1-3
- 148 1 Chronicles 4-6
- 149 1 Chronicles 7-9
- 150 1 Chronicles 10-12
- 151 1 Chronicles 13-16
- 152 1 Chronicles 17-20
- 153 1 Chronicles 21-22
- 154 1 Chronicles 23-26
- 155 1 Chronicles 27-29
- 156 2 Chronicles 1-3
- 157 2 Chronicles 4-6
- 158 2 Chronicles 7-9
- 159 Song of Solomon 1-3
- 160 Song of Solomon 4-8
- 161 Proverbs 1-3
- 162 Proverbs 4-7
- 163 Proverbs 8-11
- 164 Proverbs 12-15
- 165 Proverbs 16-19
- 166 Proverbs 20-21
- 167 Proverbs 22-24
- 168 Proverbs 25-27
- 169 Proverbs 28-29
- 170 Proverbs 30-31
- 171 Ecclesiastes 1-6
- 172 Ecclesiastes 7-12
- 173 1 Kings 4-7
- 174 1 Kings 8-9
- 175 1 Kings 10-11

- ☐ 176 1 Kings 12-15
- ☐ 177 1 Kings 16-18
- ☐ 178 1 Kings 19-22
- ☐ 179 2 Chronicles 10-13
- ☐ 180 2 Chronicles 14-16
- ☐ 181 2 Chronicles 17-18
- ☐ 182 2 Kings 1-3
- ☐ 183 2 Chronicles 19-21
- ☐ 184 2 Kings 4-6
- ☐ 185 2 Kings 7-10
- ☐ 186 Joel
- ☐ 187 2 Chronicles 22-25
- ☐ 188 2 Kings 11-14
- ☐ 189 Jonah
- ☐ 190 Amos 1-3
- ☐ 191 Amos 4-6
- ☐ 192 Amos 7-9
- ☐ 193 2 Chronicles 26-29
- ☐ 194 2 Kings 15-17
- ☐ 195 2 Kings 18-20
- ☐ 196 2 Chronicles 30-32
- ☐ 197 Isaiah 36-39
- ☐ 198 2 Kings 21
- ☐ 199 Hosea 1-4
- ☐ 200 Hosea 5-9
- ☐ 201 Hosea 10-14
- ☐ 202 Micah 1-4
- ☐ 203 Micah 5-7
- ☐ 204 Isaiah 1-3
- ☐ 205 Isaiah 4-6
- ☐ 206 Isaiah 7-8
- ☐ 207 Isaiah 9-10
- ☐ 208 Isaiah 11-15
- ☐ 209 Isaiah 16-18
- ☐ 210 Isaiah 19-22
- ☐ 211 Isaiah 23-26
- ☐ 212 Isaiah 27-29
- ☐ 213 Isaiah 30-33
- ☐ 214 Isaiah 34-35
- ☐ 215 Isaiah 40-41
- ☐ 216 Isaiah 42-43
- ☐ 217 Isaiah 44-48
- ☐ 218 Isaiah 49-51
- ☐ 219 Isaiah 52-54
- ☐ 220 Isaiah 55-58
- ☐ 221 Isaiah 59-60
- ☐ 222 Isaiah 61-64
- ☐ 223 Isaiah 65-66
- ☐ 224 Nahum
- ☐ 225 Zephaniah
- ☐ 226 Habakkuk
- ☐ 227 Obadiah
- ☐ 228 2 Kings 22-25
- ☐ 229 2 Chronicles 33-36
- ☐ 230 Jeremiah 1-3
- ☐ 231 Jeremiah 4-5
- ☐ 232 Jeremiah 6-8
- ☐ 233 Jeremiah 9-12
- ☐ 234 Jeremiah 13-16
- ☐ 235 Jeremiah 17-20
- ☐ 236 Jeremiah 21-24
- ☐ 237 Jeremiah 25-27
- ☐ 238 Jeremiah 28-30
- ☐ 239 Jeremiah 31-32
- ☐ 240 Jeremiah 33-36
- ☐ 241 Jeremiah 37-40
- ☐ 242 Jeremiah 41-43
- ☐ 243 Jeremiah 44-48
- ☐ 244 Jeremiah 49
- ☐ 245 Jeremiah 50
- ☐ 246 Jeremiah 51-52
- ☐ 247 Lamentations
- ☐ 248 Ezekiel 1-3
- ☐ 249 Ezekiel 4-7
- ☐ 250 Ezekiel 8-10
- ☐ 251 Ezekiel 11-15
- ☐ 252 Ezekiel 16-17
- ☐ 253 Ezekiel 18-21
- ☐ 254 Ezekiel 22-24
- ☐ 255 Ezekiel 25-28
- ☐ 256 Ezekiel 29-31
- ☐ 257 Ezekiel 32-33
- ☐ 258 Ezekiel 34-36
- ☐ 259 Ezekiel 37-39
- ☐ 260 Ezekiel 40-42
- ☐ 261 Ezekiel 43-45
- ☐ 262 Ezekiel 46-48
- ☐ 263 Daniel 1-3
- ☐ 264 Daniel 4-6
- ☐ 265 Daniel 7-9
- ☐ 266 Daniel 10-12
- ☐ 267 Ezra 1-5
- ☐ 268 Haggai
- ☐ 269 Zechariah 1-5
- ☐ 270 Zechariah 6-9
- ☐ 271 Zechariah 10-14
- ☐ 272 Ezra 6-10
- ☐ 273 Nehemiah 1-4
- ☐ 274 Nehemiah 5-8
- ☐ 275 Nehemiah 9-10
- ☐ 276 Nehemiah 11-13
- ☐ 277 Esther 1-6
- ☐ 278 Esther 7-10
- ☐ 279 Malachi
- ☐ 280 Matthew 1-3
- ☐ 281 Matthew 4-8
- ☐ 282 Matthew 9-11
- ☐ 283 Matthew 12-13
- ☐ 284 Matthew 14-16
- ☐ 285 Matthew 17-20
- ☐ 286 Matthew 21-24
- ☐ 287 Matthew 25-28
- ☐ 288 Mark 1-3
- ☐ 289 Mark 4-5
- ☐ 290 Mark 6-9
- ☐ 291 Mark 10-13
- ☐ 292 Mark 14-16
- ☐ 293 Luke 1-3
- ☐ 294 Luke 4-6
- ☐ 295 Luke 7-9
- ☐ 296 Luke 10-13
- ☐ 297 Luke 14-16
- ☐ 298 Luke 17-19
- ☐ 299 Luke 20-22
- ☐ 300 Luke 23-24
- ☐ 301 John 1-3
- ☐ 302 John 4-5
- ☐ 303 John 6-7
- ☐ 304 John 8-9
- ☐ 305 John 10-12
- ☐ 306 John 13-17
- ☐ 307 John 18-19
- ☐ 308 John 20-21
- ☐ 309 Acts 1-3
- ☐ 310 Acts 4-6
- ☐ 311 Acts 7-9
- ☐ 312 Acts 10-12
- ☐ 313 Acts 13-14
- ☐ 314 Acts 15
- ☐ 315 James
- ☐ 316 Galatians 1-3
- ☐ 317 Galatians 4-6
- ☐ 318 Acts 16-18
- ☐ 319 1 Thessalonians
- ☐ 320 2 Thessalonians
- ☐ 321 1 Corinthians 1-5
- ☐ 322 1 Corinthians 6-9
- ☐ 323 1 Corinthians 10-11
- ☐ 324 1 Corinthians 12-13
- ☐ 325 1 Corinthians 14
- ☐ 326 1 Corinthians 15-16
- ☐ 327 2 Corinthians 1-3
- ☐ 328 2 Corinthians 4-7
- ☐ 329 2 Corinthians 8-10
- ☐ 330 2 Corinthians 11-13
- ☐ 331 Acts 19-20
- ☐ 332 Romans 1-4
- ☐ 333 Romans 5-8
- ☐ 334 Romans 9-12
- ☐ 335 Romans 13-16
- ☐ 336 Acts 21-24
- ☐ 337 Acts 25-26
- ☐ 338 Acts 27-28
- ☐ 339 Ephesians 1-3
- ☐ 340 Ephesians 4-6
- ☐ 341 Colossians
- ☐ 342 Philemon- Philip.1
- ☐ 343 Philippians 2-4
- ☐ 344 Titus - 1 Peter 1
- ☐ 345 1 Peter 2-5
- ☐ 346 1 Timothy 1-3
- ☐ 347 1 Timothy 4-6
- ☐ 348 2 Peter
- ☐ 349 2 Timothy
- ☐ 350 Hebrews 1-4
- ☐ 351 Hebrews 5-8
- ☐ 352 Hebrews 9-10
- ☐ 353 Hebrews 11-13
- ☐ 354 Jude - 1 John 1-2
- ☐ 355 1 John 3-5
- ☐ 356 2 John - 3 John
- ☐ 357 Revelation 1-3
- ☐ 358 Revelation 4-6
- ☐ 359 Revelation 7-9
- ☐ 360 Revelation 10-12
- ☐ 361 Revelation 13-15
- ☐ 362 Revelation 16-18
- ☐ 363 Revelation 19-22